A DISCOURSE ON NOVELTY AND CREATION

SUNY Series in Philosophy
Robert C. Neville, Editor

A Discourse on Novelty and Creation

Carl R. Hausman

STATE UNIVERSITY NEW YORK PRESS

ALBANY

Published by
State University of New York Press, Albany
© 1984 State University of New York
All rights reserved
Printed in the United States of America

No part of this book may be used or reproduced in any manner whatsoever without written permission except in the case of brief quotations embodied in critical articles and reviews.

For information, address State University of New York Press, State University Plaza, Albany, NY 12246

Library of Congress Cataloging in Publication Data

Hausman, Carl R.
   A discourse on novelty and creation.

   (SUNY series in philosophy)
   Originally published: The Hague: M. Nijhoff, 1975.
   Includes bibliographical refrences and index.
   1. Creative ability. I. Title. II. Series.
BF408.H317 1984   153.3'5   83-17986
ISBM 0-87395-864-0
ISBN 0-87395-865-9 (pbk.)

10 9 8 7 6 5 4 3 2 1

PREFACE

Over the past two decades, the number of studies of creativity has increased enormously. Although these studies represent a wide variety of perspectives, the largest proportion of them falls within the province of the social and behavioral sciences. Perhaps this is due to the impetus of experimental psychologists, who recognized the special problems that arise when originality is treated under a general theory of cognition. But whatever the reason, human creativity has come to be viewed as one of the major concerns of the twentieth century. It has been referred to as the most pressing problem of our time.

In spite of the importance of the topic, few philosophers have either analyzed or speculated systematically about creativity, as a distinct topic. This neglect may be the expression of a tacit and sometimes explicit conviction that creativity must be taken for granted and not subjected to analytic scrutiny. In any case, the determination of so many behavioral and social scientists not to fall behind in the search for understanding creativity has led to a proliferation of publications that are unrelated to one another and that lack clearly ordered and reflective consideration of what creativity is. Too few writers have either acknowledged or examined what they presuppose about creative acts, about human activity, and about the nature of explanation when they focus on so complex a phenomenon as creativity.

I believe that philosophy has much to contribute to the examination of these presuppositions. A philosophical perspective on them can shed light on creativity in a way that may be of help to scientific as well as to humanistic understanding. Indeed, it seems to me that philosophical reflections are essential to providing a clarity and an order that is now absent. My own reflections have been in evolution for a decade or more. I offer them in this book with the hope of contributing a rather neglected dimension to the understanding of creative activity.

My interest in creativity originated in issues appropriate to the branch of philosophy called "aesthetics," or more precisely, "philosophy of art." Of the many problems raised by philosophers of art, two are especially relevant to the topic of creativity – those focused on the activity of the artist and those focused on the work of art as a product of that activity. Questions about the artist and his work have been central to my own initial interest in the philosophy of art. Specifically, I was intrigued by two questions: Under what conditions do works of art seem valuable? and Under what conditions are those works creations rather than mere products? My conception of these questions has been refined and modified as I have come to see their connection with a complex of other problems – for instance, problems involved in understanding the aesthetic experience of the spectator of art and the relation of such experience to that of the creator, the question of the relation of aesthetic to moral value, and the relation of value judgments to various kinds of art criticism. More generally, and for me most significantly, the two questions which initiated my interests lead inevitably to questions about the relation of explanation in the study of art to explanation in other fields and, in turn, to questions about a more comprehensive view of man and his place in the world. These larger questions have guided my reflections about creativity.

There is a sense in which the two questions in their initial form remain the key to the development of the main themes of this book. My view that there are ineradicable limitations on understanding creativity and value depends upon facing certain peculiarities and difficulties one encounters in studying this topic. Further, the consequences of acknowledging these limitations suggest a number of conclusions about the nature of knowledge and about what we can know in the broadest sense, since the limitations point to the elusiveness of experience and its intelligibility in general. At the same time, I see no way of elucidating and clarifying the topic of creativity, whether for practical or for purely theoretical purposes, without constructing a conceptual scheme which can serve as a basis for a qualified understanding of creative acts.

The construction of such a scheme is my final aim. However, my most immediate concern is to offer the following discussion as a step toward clarifying the uniqueness of the difficulties investigators face in treating creativity. I hope to bring into relief presuppositions too often overlooked by those who study this topic. Thus, in emphasizing the peculiarities and puzzling features of creativity, I share something with the relatively new tradition of existential philosophy, especially in its insistence upon the absolute uniqueness and freedom of certain human acts. It seems to me that one of the contributions of this tradition lies in its reminding us of the autonomy of human beings in their individuality as opposed to the inevitable regularities and logical or dialectical necessities that have served philosophy and science so extensively as models for the rational understanding of man and the world. Yet even though I want to show that creativity cannot be reduced to a system of laws, I also wish to avoid reducing creativity to a mystery that defies speech and all forms of understanding. Creativity is not one among a series of natural conditions or kinds of events in a system; nor is it something we know not what, which violates our intelligible grasp of experience. Rather, creativity must be understood in the light of both these alternatives as well as from a unique perspective.

SECOND PREFACE

The second publication of a book offers the opportunity to correct, revise, and develop the discussion of an author's ideas. I shall not take advantage of this opportunity. The text remains almost completely untouched. It remains so not because I am so conceited as to think there are no faults in the discussion. Nor is it because my thought about the problems of creativity has undergone no evolution since 1975. Certainly the book is neither faultless nor a final statement. However, upon reflection, I cannot but stand by the substance of the discourse offered in the present text. Where the discussion might ask most urgently for development, what is needed demands the initiation of a new direction rather than an extension of what is there. For instance, a thesis about the referential function of metaphor which I have proposed in other manuscripts written since the publication of this book would extend the claim about the relation of creativity to metaphor. And the ontology that is adumbrated in the last chapter is matter for another work. The last chapter after all was intended primarily as a way of pointing to the direction of ontology suggested by the consequences of what I say about creative achievements.

In spite of my resistance to developing the thought as it stands, I cannot resist commenting briefly on issues raised by two readers who offered several critical observations about the argument. The first issue concerns what I say about why one must place limitations on what we can expect of explanations of creativity. The first two chapters of the book include discussions of this issue. The second two chapters explore consequences of this discussion. The contention that there are limitations on explaining creativity, then, is fundamental and pervasive and I would hope that my reasons for being skeptical about explanation are at least clear, even if they might be challenged.

Part of my argument adopted the language of causality. My intention was to show that those who want to explain creativity may assume that the result of a creative process is an effect of necessary and sufficient causes that are antecedently "given." In such a causal relation, I suggested, a cause includes all that is needed to understand all those aspects of the effect that we expect to make it intelligible as an effect. In making my point this way, one might say that I have presupposed that effects (in this case created outcomes) resemble their causes. The picture one could build here, I suppose, is of effects construed as replicas of the cause. Of course, this is not a picture of explanation that satisfies contemporary theorists of explanation in most philosophical circles—even those that fall outside the analytic tradition. However, what needs to be made clear is that a causal view of explanation sets a framework for ways of denying that there is anything new under the sun. A classical deterministic approach denies this in a way that assumes a causal chain within which everything subsequent to any point in the chain is necessitated. Thus no spontaneity is possible. However, whether effects resemble causes is not the issue. What is at issue is whether every significant aspect of the effect of a cause could have been predicted if the predictor had enough knowledge of the cause and the circumstances under which the cause functions. If a person who had been creative in the past were to begin work on a painting or a poem, could a predictor tell us what qualities, what specific form and content, and what value would be expected in the painting or the poem? The issue centers on predictability, not resemblances between effects and causes, and the question need not be formulated in terms of causal relations, though this is the formulation that has come to us from the past. But if the issue is viewed in terms of predictability, it is crucial that we see what is included in the concept of predictability. Since we are dealing with created outcomes which are unfamiliar and intelligible, we cannot avoid including in the prediction references to the unique ordering of the aspects of those outcomes. To have predicted *that* Picasso would produce in any given year or month is not to predict what the painting's form and content would be, not even whether it would merit being seen as creatively produced— though this would be likely, given Picasso's success in the past. But if we believed our prediction is a sign that we have explained creativity, then the prediction would need to inform us of the aspects of the effect (the painting) that render it both new and intelligible. And this necessarily would include the unique aspects of the effect. It is not resemblance but rather predictability of the traits (the crucial ones that make it intelligible) which is in question.

A second issue has been raised from two divergent perspectives. What kind of discourse is most appropriate for a discussion of creativity? The discourse I have used in this book might be regarded on the one hand as "tight" and analytical and on the other hand as loose in resorting to metaphor and to the use of unfamiliar terms in familiar contexts and familiar terms in unfamiliar contexts. Which one of these two characteristics of the text is present—or whether they both are present—must be left to the reader. What is perceived as the presence or the dominance of one or the other will depend, I suspect, on the reader's philosophical perspective. My own appraisal leads me to conclude that the proper discourse for the topic of creativity cannot be that of a monolithic style or method of articulating the points that need to be made. One should not strive for impressionistic observation and perhaps would-be poetry of some sort. What is needed is sober examination of an elusive phenomenon. But one should not therefore expect to subject the phenomenon under consideration completely to strict analytic tools. Analysis, I think, reaches its limits just as explanation does. And when this limit is reached, language must be used so that familiar terms—*form, structure, novelty, causality,* for instance—are used in unusual contexts and unfamiliar terms—*Novelty Proper, the value of beings* (*as such*), for example—appear in contexts of normal usage. If stretching language to fit the elusiveness of the phenomenon is to succeed, however, metaphorical expressions must also enter an account of creativity. The problem of this kind of search for reflective understanding of creativity and a world that includes it is consedered in the last two chapters of this book. And again, I am prepared to stand by the substance of what I said there.

State College, Pennsylvania
November, 1983

ACKNOWLEDGMENTS

My reflections are based upon a series of papers which I have published over the past ten years. The Introduction brings together with some revision portions of the first chapter of my monograph, "The Existence of Novelty" and a paper, "Mystery, Paradox, and the Creative Act." [1] The first chapter is a slightly revised version of "Form, Value, and Novelty in the Creative Process." [2] Chapter II is based on my paper, "Spontaneity: Its Arationality and Its Reality." [3] Chapter III merges a paper, "The Phenomenon of Originative Speech" with the second chapter of the monograph referred to above.[4] In merging these, I have expanded and revised the original discussion. The fourth chapter is a development of some of the ideas in a paper entitled, "Intelligibility and the Existentially Absurd." [5] I wish to express my appreciation to the editors of *International Philosophical Quarterly, Pacific Philosophy Forum, The Philosophy Forum,* and *The Southern Journal of Philosophy* for the use of the articles which are the basis for chapters in this book. Also, for the use of my paper in *New Essays in Phenomenology* (Copyright© 1969), I should like to thank Quadrangle/The New York Times Book Co., and for the use of my paper in *Essays in Metaphysics,* I should like to thank The Pennsylvania State University Press. I am grateful to Random House – Alfred A. Knopf,

---

[1] "The Existence of Novelty," *Pacific Philosophy Forum,* Vol. 4, No. 3, pp. 4-60. "Mystery, Paradox, and the Creative Act." *the Southern Journal of Philosophy,* Vol. 7, No. 3, pp. 289-296.
[2] "Form, Value, and Novelty in the Creative Process," in *Essays in Metaphysics,* edited by Carl G. Vaught (University Park and London: The Pennsylvania State University Press, 1970), pp. 79-103.
[3] "Spontaneity: Its Arationality and Its Reality," *International Philosophical Quarterly,* Vol. IV, No. 1, pp. 2-47.
[4] "The Phenomenon of Originative Speech," *The Philosophy Forum,* Vol. 7, No. 4, pp. 45-55.
[5] "Intelligibility and the Existentially Absurd," in *New Essays in Phenomenology* (Chicago: Quadrangle Books, 1969) pp. 212-230.

Inc., for permission to quote from Wallace Stevens, *Opus Posthumous*, edited by Samuel French Morse (Copyright© 1957).

I should like to express my gratitude to the American Philosophical Society for two summer grants, in 1964 and 1965, to support the writing of the monograph, "The Existence of Novelty" and the writing of the essay, "Form, Value, and Novelty in the Creative Process." Also, I am grateful for assistance from the Central Fund for Research, The Pennsylvania State University, in preparing this manuscript for publication.

It would be futile to attempt to acknowledge the full extent of my indebtedness to colleagues and teachers. However, I must mention the names of several persons without whose encouragement, moral support, and critical help this volume would not have been completed. My teacher, Eliseo Vivas is responsible for the inspiration which initiated my study of creativity. Of course, the turn which my thought has taken should not be traced to him, and I should emphasize the obvious point that whatever errors may be present in my thought are solely my responsibility. Others to whom I am grateful for their criticisms and encouragement are John Anderson, Richard Bernstein, Brand Blanshard, James Daley, Stanley Rosen, Albert Rothenberg, John. E. Smith, Carl Vaught, and Donald Verene. Finally, I want to acknowledge the extent to which a number of students in several of my seminars have contributed to the perspective and the stimulation so important in the articulation of the view presented in this book.

CONTENTS

INTRODUCTION: THE PROBLEM, ITS BACKGROUND, AND A SKETCH OF ITS TREATMENT ... 1

I. PRODUCTION AND RADICAL CREATION ... 18
   A. Novelty Proper ... 19
      1. Individuality and Radical Newness ... 19
      2. Form ... 30
         a. Form, structures, and valuation ... 30
         b. Form and novelty, some problems and puzzles ... 33
   B. Novelty Proper and Creative Acts ... 39
      1. Imitation and Craftsmanship ... 40
      2. Creative Process and Critical Control ... 41
      3. Creative Achievement and Duplication of Novelty ... 44
   C. Value and Creativity ... 46
      1. Instrumental Value ... 47
      2. Instrumental Value and Tradition ... 48
      3. Inerent Value ... 49

II. SPONTANEITY: THE PARADOX AND THE POSSIBILITY OF EXPLANATION ... 53
   A. General Remarks about Explanation ... 55
   B. The Paradox of Creativity ... 59
      1. Whitehead and Explanation ... 60
      2. The Paradox in the Context of the Husserlian Account of Consciousness ... 64
      3. Nicolai Hartmann's Acknowledgement of the Radical Puzzle ... 64
   C. The Reality of Spontaneity and the Challenge of Determinism ... 68
      1. Positivism ... 70
      2. Teleological Determinism ... 72
      3. Mechanistic Determinism ... 74
   D. Intelligibility and the Resources of Language ... 81

III.	LANGUAGE AND THE AESTHETIC STRUCTURE OF NOVELTY	85
	A. Originative Speech as Oblique Expression	86
	1. Language and Speech	86
	2. Speech and Implements	91
	B. Speech and Metaphors	93
	1. Indirect Speech and Metaphor in Art, Science, and Philosophy	93
	2. Metaphors and the Organic Character of Art	96
	3. Metaphors as Constitutive Negations	99
	4. Metaphors and "Family Resemblances"	110
	C. Metaphors and the Intelligibility of Created Objects	114
	1. Metaphorical Expression and Paradox	115
	2. The Structure of Novelty	116
	3. Intelligibility and Familiarity	118
IV.	FUNDAMENTAL PARADOX AND INTELLIGIBILITY	124
	A. The Absurd	126
	B. Two Loci of the Absurd	131
	C. The Second Model of Intelligibility	138
	D. The Possibility of a Third Model of Intelligibility	145
INDEX		156

INTRODUCTION:
THE PROBLEM, ITS BACKGROUND,
AND A SKETCH OF ITS TREATMENT

Creative activity seems almost magical in its power to fascinate us. Such fascination is evoked whether creative acts are regarded as orderly and predictable events or as radical, unprecedented transformations in what we experience. Occurrences of what appears to be new have appealed to the imagination and have challenged the curiosity of reflective persons throughout the history of thought. For some, creativity has seemed awesome. At the very least, it has been puzzling to most inquirers who have asked about the basis and origin of objects and events, or of the world itself.

Although creativity has been a fascination throughout the history of Western thought, interest in it has recently blossomed. Since the nineteenth century, when Romanticism developed in the arts and Idealism in philosophy, creativity has attracted special attention. Romanticism has stressed the right and need of the artist to be free of established rules and the exigencies of his artistic tradition; Idealism has emphasized the constitutive function of the mind in knowing and the creative advance of man and the world toward new stages of development. In our own times, a high premium is placed on creative activity in all areas of life. Not only does creativity on the part of man as well as nature fascinate us, but it also calls forth admiration and praise. Originality is virtually a *sine qua non* of value in art and, indeed, in all humanistic endeavor. Innovation in the sciences is regarded both as necessary and as a mark of greatness. And in politics and morality, creativity (if its consequences seem successful) incites respect as it does in the arts and the sciences.

If admiration for creative activity has recently intensified, puzzlement about its occurrences also has recently come into focus as a special problem. This puzzlement has taken many forms and has led to a number of distinguishable problems. These problems generally concern the motives which drive a human being to create, the possibility that there are special personality traits which distinguish creative persons, and the stages that can be discriminated within creative processes. However, one problem focuses what is most puzzling to inquirers: Can creativity be explained? This problem is central. Not only is an answer to it the basis for answering the other questions, but it expresses the earliest as well as the most recent fascination with the problem change. Concern about explanation lies at the heart of the recognition of creative activity as puzzling.

The notion that creativity is in some sense problematic is related to the hope that all of our experience can be understood. The appearance of the unexpected, the occurrence of a phenomenon which does not fit into a niche in the scheme of things, presents a puzzle for our conceptual grasp of the world. We want to know how something not apparently required by our categories of understanding can suddenly – or gradually – come into being. It is the desire to understand this puzzle that has led philosophers to inquire into the origin of novelty, into the conditions and laws by virtue of which novel objects or events as well as ideas issue from natural and human activities. Of course, interest in the problem of whether creativity can be explained has taken different forms in different historical periods and, at least until the nineteenth century, the interest in explaining it has been subordinated to the broader purposes of understanding reality itself. Yet even though creativity has not been viewed as a topic in its own right, there are distinguishable philosophical perspectives on the phenomenon as a problem to be reckoned with in the understanding of the nature of things. In the remainder of this Introduction, it will be helpful to survey these perspectives and to consider them in the light of the position I shall propose as a basis for developing the topic.

It is possible to distinguish two fundamental perspectives. The first is governed by a rationalistic conviction that creativity can be explained to the extent that any kind of thing or event can be explained. Accordingly, inquiry is directed toward finding a source or foundation for creative acts, an aim most recently based upon a practical interest in identifying laws and antecedent conditions which would make creative acts predictable. The scope and precision of the predictability required may vary, but ideally, successful results of inquiry would permit prediction of who will create and what will be created such that the effects of the creation on a tradition and on society are foreseen.

The second perspective is rooted in the belief that an explanation of creativity has not been found. In its extreme form, this perspective is expressed in the conviction that a natural explanation will never be found. Accordingly, creative activity is viewed as a kind of process which necessarily eludes ordinary rational principles. Creation is thought to be a mystery for finite, human knowledge. And the proper approach to it consists essentially in an acknowledgement and an admiration of the mystery.

I believe both of these perspectives are misdirected; for both expect too much of explanation and too little of the creative act. They fail to give creativity its proper place in the world. And they fail to do so because they do not admit the possibility of another way of understanding creativity – a way which, I shall propose, indicates that creativity is paradoxical. One of the reasons why the possibility of alternative ways of understanding has not ordinarily been a key in approaching creativity, especially from the rationalist perspective, lies in the fact that too little attention has been given to characterizing creations and the acts that give rise to them. In turn, the presence and possible admissibility of paradox in such a characterization has been overlooked. In the following survey of the two fundamental perspectives or approaches to creativity, I shall anticipate the chapters to follow by further developing the point that each approach is limited. In addition, I shall suggest that a more adequate approach must be based on a view that makes room for a kind of understanding not bound by the demand that explanation include predictability. Such a view must acknowledge paradox as an inescapable feature of the world.

Let us look somewhat more closely at the two opposed perspectives on the possibility of explaining creative acts. These opposed views reflect two traditions in the history of thought, a rationalistic determinism and what, for want of a more precise term, will be call a non-rationalistic, anti-determinism. The prefix "non" is intended to indicate that the main thrust of this second tradition is contrary, though not necessarily contradictory, to the rationalistic view about what is understandable. I want to avoid suggesting that the non-rationalistic tradition wholly repudiates rational understanding at all levels.[1] My identification of these traditions,

---

[1] It should be obvious to anyone familiar with philosophical traditions that I must use the term "rationalist" in the broadest possible sense to refer to any approach that views experience as understandable through principles and (at least in part) conceptual schemes. Admissible principles may themselves transcend conceptualization, as they do when merged in the notion of Substance or God for Spinoza. But such principles would be accepted as relevant to understanding experience because they are thought to be necessary as components of, or as the foundation of, a system. They are thus deemed reasonable in some sense in order to make experience intelligible. Such reasonableness may be elusive, requiring divine as well as natural reason for full access to it. But the inclusion of reason in some form is crucial in distinguishing this general perspective in philosophy from avowed mysticism and forms of irrationalism. In any case, the term "rationalist" is intended to cover diverse positions including metaphysical systems that admit a divine source, and empiricism for which reason may be viewed in terms of habits and regularities in sense experience.

to be sure, is an oversimplification. There are many versions and overlapping variations within them. However, I think that the labels I use do cover all variations relevant to the fundamental perspectives on explaining creativity.

Although I shall not attempt to identify the many versions of rationalism and its contrary, it is necessary to outline the most general of these variations. I shall refer to two versions of rationalism: naturalism and supernaturalism. Naturalism includes on the one hand experimental science and on the other hand more speculative approaches, such as those of "depth psychology" and materialism, that admit principles or concepts applicable to something that does not transcend nature but may transcend finite human consciousness as well as observable behavior.[2] Supernaturalism can take two directions. Its proponents may affirm that an explanatory divine source is intelligible in principle and thus not fundamentally mysterious. This version remains rationalistic. The other version is non-rationalistic or trans-rationalistic; it affirms that the divine source of creativity is itself ultimately unintelligible or mysterious. Both supernaturalisms will be described somewhat more fully below.

Naturalism is the more rigorous and more recent version of the rationalist tradition. On this view, creative acts are conceived as natural events that are intelligible just as are other events in nature. They occur as moments of natural processes, and they can be described in the same terms as can all natural processes. The naturalistic interpretation of creativity stems most directly from the thought of Aristotle. According to Aristotle, the art process consists in making something which exhibits a form imposed upon a material.[3] What Aristotle meant by this, of course,

[2] B. F. Skinner has recently stated in a popular lecture, "On Having a Poem," *Saturday Review*, Vol. LV, No. 29 (July, 1972), a view of creativity that seems to me to illustrate clearly that the approach of experimental scientists to creativity falls under the general perspective of rationalism. Skinner proposes the view that poets are like instruments conditioned by heredity and environment to write just what they write. He compares their lack of responsibility for what they produce with the lack of responsibility of a mother in deciding what the features of her infant child will be when it is born. Creativity is to be accounted for by reference to conditions independent of, but correlated with, the creator who is viewed as a complex of responses to these conditions. This is one form of determinism. There are other examples, of course, and Skinner's popular, and in this instance superficial, statement is hardly startling. But it is evidence that my discussion of naturalistic rationalism, and determinism, is not of a view that no one holds any longer.

[3] This account of Aristotle's interpretation is based specifically on what he says in *Metaphysics* 1032a-1034a. There are other statements in Aristotle that are particularly suggestive for the topic of creativity in its contemporary form, especially his discussion of change in *Physics* 196b-198a. It might seem an egregious oversight not to refer also to *Poetics*. However, I take *Poetics* to be an application of Aristotle's conception of the art process, an application concerned primarily with what distinguishes among art forms and with what accounts for aesthetic judgment.

is more complex than the literal interpretation of it that has been influential on classical theories of art. In any case, as the basis for the naturalistic tradition, Aristotle's view suggests that the form is like a preconceived plan according to which a material is fashioned. The preconceived form functions something like a design which is represented by a blueprint. It implies the rules for making the product, and it results from conditions under which the creator interacts with the world. As a natural agent, he is a constituent within a natural process which develops according to a determinate principle of order. Hence, the product of his activity is an effect that is brought about in accordance with a predetermined logic.

As already suggested, this naturalistic interpretation presupposes that originality is predictable in principle. Further, predictions must offer more than the trivial expectation that if a person has been creative in the past he will create something in the future – though exactly what the creation will be remains to be seen. The naturalistic position depends on the possibility that prediction of the essential features – and perhaps all features – of creations would be possible if all relevant natural (including human) factors could be identified. Such complete knowledge would constitute an explanation. And the possibility of such an explanation implies that the individual agent is not a source of creativity, but, at best, is one among a complex series of other natural conditions for the creative act.

The opposed interpretation of creativity, which denies that creativity can be rationally explained, derives most directly from one interpretation of Plato's writings about art. Plato was the first writer in the Western tradition known to have explored the issue of how rhapsodes and poets – or how those who today are thought of as creative artists – articulate ideas and feelings which cannot be accounted for in what they have learned. And it was Plato who explicitly proposed the view that the poet (creator) works by inspiration. As inspired, the poet is out of his mind. He is out of his mind in the sense that what he does is not the result of what is present in his experience before he originates the novel product. While engaged in the act of creation, he is not in full control of himself. He is a spokesman for a source beyond his own conscious mental activity. On Plato's view, the mark of originality is a kind of divine madness.[4]

It should be clear why the view of creativity that appeals to divine madness, or to inspiration from a source outside the creator, has been

---

[4] Although Plato's view of issues relevant to creativity are present in a number of his dialogues, one dialogue in particular, the *Ion*, raises the question of understanding the process of creativity and accounting for works of art that cannot be reduced to craft or a fund of knowledge available outside art. In the *Phaedrus,* Plato also speaks of the poet's divine madness.

associated with the view that creativity is mysterious. If the act of creation is not wholly controlled by the creator himself, and if something crucial in what does control it is not present in the conditions of nature, but rather has its origin in a divine power or super-human agency, then explanation in terms of human understanding is placed in question, if not denied. Prediction of the outcome of a creative act is impossible, in the absence of prior knowledge about the plan for the work and the rules necessary to carry out this plan. But if the source of the plan is transcendent with respect to human conditions, then finite, human knowledge is limited with respect to gaining access to the plan – unless, of course, some form of supernatural knowledge is possible.[5]

However, it should be observed that in spite of the limitation placed on explanation by the perspective that can be traced to Plato, one version of this perspective shares a commitment with naturalism and thereby bears a kinship with the tradition of rationalism. In looking to a source beyond the finite creator, at bottom an appeal is made to a principle or ground, which, if understood, would make creative acts fully rational. Thus, the source of creative acts is mysterious for *us*; but it need not be mysterious from the point of view of itself, i.e., from the standpoint of the rationality of the ultimate source. If human knowledge were not finite, but could transcend itself and be adequate to the source, creativity would be fully understood.

The point I want to make about the appeal to an ultimate source is crucial. In the first place, I want to insist that not only rationalism, but also a version of supernaturalism, which might be taken as a form of non-rationalism, may be committed to affirming the possibility that creativity is explicable. In the second place, I want to emphasize that a supernaturalism is non-rationalistic only if it affirms a mystery in the divine source, and a mystery which even divinity does not make reasonable. Both forms of supernaturalism, I think, can be traced to the influence of Plato. But whatever their origin, they both, as either rationalist or non-rationalist, minimize the power of a finite agency to create in its own terms. Both rationalism and non-rationalism overlook the human agent as a primary source of the creative act.

---

[5] One twentieth century illustration of the appeal to divinity is found in Jacques Maritain's interesting and sensitive work, *Creative Intuition in Art and Poetry*. (New York: Bollingen Series, Pantheon Books, 1963). Maritain offers an account of the poetic process in its most basic level, which is beyond observable behavior. But he also traces the power of this process to divinity, at which point he ceases to offer an explanation.

Before pursuing this point further, however, it is in order to suggest the reason I shall bring into question the naturalistic or, more broadly, the rationalistic perspective on creativity. This reason is grounded in the character of created objects – in the newness or the increment of novelty that marks a product as one which is created. I believe that the presence of novelty in the created object implies that an unresolvable paradox is an inevitable condition of creative acts. It is this unresolvable paradox to which both rationalistic and non-rationalistic approaches fail to do justice.

Let me elaborate this suggestion. The most obvious evidence that an object is created is that it seems different from anything that was known before its occurrence. But merely being different is not a guarantee of creativity. If novelty consisted only in difference, then every distinct thing we know or could know would be novel. All things would be viewed as products of creativity and creativity would be found everywhere; for, on this interpretation, each object in the world is a singular or individual thing. As such, each thing can be encountered in its own terms, as just whatever it happens to be, and as different from every other thing. Two grains of sand, no matter how much one is like the other, are not identical, even if they share all their discernible qualities. If they were identical, they would be one and not two. Further, on the closest inspection, minute differences between them can be detected – for instance, subtle variations on the surfaces, impurities in the material, slight differences in their weights, etc. Each is unique and different from all other things. Newness in the sense of uniqueness is universally present as a created character in all things.

The view that creativity pervades all things is attractive, for it invites us to treat each experience as fresh and potentially significant in unexpected ways. It sugests that if we attend to the uniquenesses of things, we become participants in the creativity of the world. In thus responding to things, our experience has a kind of novelty, and because we are responsible for our responses, we are partially (if not wholly) responsible for the uniqueness we find.

However, as provocative and valuable as this view may be, it does not do justice to the more striking and profound occurrences of creativity – to instances that exemplify the kind of freshness or novelty that surpasses the individuality common to all things. What can be said about those processes that lead to products which not only are unique as individuals, but also, as new, contribute in new ways to the advance of a tradition of art, science, or to evolution in nature? It is these more radical changes – those which lead to new developments in the world – that we attribute to genius.

And it is interest in these dramatic instances that initiated attempts to understand creativity.

This point does not necessitate excluding attention to less dramatic achievements found in such areas as cookery, child rearing, and the various crafts. Much recent inquiry has been concerned with such activities and has emphasized the need to gain knowledge about these in order both to understand the creative abilities of eminent persons – those exhibiting dramatic creativity – and to promote creative activity in all persons.[6] However, as important as these concerns are, the adequacy of the results of inquiry about creativity depends upon testing the results in the light of the kind of activity that leads to products that are more than unusual or merely different and that have called attention to extraordinary efforts and capabilities on the part of certain human beings. Without such models, we would not have been alerted to the possibility that so-called ordinary individuals have even a small degree of the potentialities prominent in extraordinary individuals. Without an appreciation of extraordinary creativity, we would not acknowledge ordinary creativity.

What, then, is the mark of this more radical newness – the newness associated with the most striking examples of creativity? An answer to this question is suggested by a closer consideration of the things regarded as creations. Whether the created thing is a physical object or mental product expressed as an image or an idea, it exhibits a newness in the intelligible character of the thing, or in what for the moment I shall refer to as the "kind" of thing it is. Radical novelty is a newness of kind.[7] Novelty of kind can be understood by contrast with the newness of singularity. A thing considered exclusively in terms of what it is as a singular or as an individual is considered simply as an isolable and discrete item in experience. But if this is the only way the thing is regarded, then that thing is not known for what it is. That is, if we take account of a thing only in terms of its being discrete, of its being simply an individual, then although we do acknowledge that it is something, we do not take account of what kind of thing it is; we ignore those characteristics it has which enable us

---

[6] A. H. Maslow, for instance, proposes such an approach in *Toward a Psychology of Being* (Princeton, New Jersey: D. Van Nostrand Co., Inc., 1962) especially pp. 127-137.
[7] In Chapter I, newness of kind will be called "Novelty Proper," a term that I first used in "The Existence of Novelty," *Pacific Philosophy Forum,* Vol. 4, No. 3 (February, 1966), pp. 4-60, but anticipated by at least one other writer. The background for the term will be mentioned later. It should be made clear that the occurrence of newness of kind, or Novelty Proper, is not sufficient to guarantee that the source of a new form is creative. Not only must certain kinds of value accompany the form, but certain conditions also must be present in the relation of the process to the future. These additional points will be discussed in the next chapter.

to identify it and give it a place among those things which we know. But a thing understood for *what* it is, as well as *that* it is, is describable and relatable to other things and to general principles; that is, it is an identity known for what it is when it is recognized as an example of some kind, when it is regarded as a particular instance of some kind of reality. Grains of sand, for example, are known for what they are because they are identifiable as kinds of things which share a certain complex of characteristics – such as solidity, shape, non-flammibility, etc. I shall later refer to such complexes of characteristics as structures and as Forms.

Novelty, then, may occur in connection with the distinguishing complex of characteristics of a thing that is thought to be created. Thus, novelty is sometimes recognized in the difference between the kind to which a thing belongs and other kinds – in the contrast between what is already identifiable and the complex of characteristics that enables us to know what the thing is which is novel. When something that occurs for the first time is an example of a kind never known before, that thing is new in a more radical or fundamental sense than novelty of sheer difference. Such novelty occurs in biological evolution. What marks a creative advance is a change which results in a different species, a different kind or Form of creature. In the history of painting, creativity most obviously occurs when a different style appears, and a different style appears when there occurs a different pattern of visual or plastic qualities in the painter's product. Of course, variations within styles may also manifest different patterns and may also be creations. Such instances will be specifically taken into account later. I am here concerned with the most obvious or readily identifiable differences in intelligible characteristics of things.

The reason we have been considering what it is for something to be new is that we were faced with the question of whether the novelty in a created object implies that creativity reveals an unavoidable paradox – a paradox for both the rationalist and the non-rationalist. What I have said should help answer this question.

First of all, it should be evident that a created object exhibits a complex structure that is new and is unprecedented and unpredicted. It appears to be unaccounted for by antecedents and available knowledge, and it is thus disconnected with its past. In this sense, it occurs in the midst of discontinuity. It is a formerly unrecognized identity, an identity that is different and that exhibits a coherence that marks it off from other identities. Of course, it is the expectation of the rationalist perspective that this discontinuity must be shown illusory or irrelevant. The new kind must be connected with its antecedents. Nevertheless, the datum does appear as a break in continuities, and it remains to be seen whether a rational understanding of it can be found, or, more fundamentally, whether such rational understanding is even possible. In any case, the discontinuity between creations and their antecedents is a peculiar discontinuity. It holds between previously known identities and identities that are strange. Moreover, the strange identities have a puzzling relation to the products in which they are found. On the one hand, the identity of a creation is a kind or a complex of characteristics that must be knowable apart from the sheer individuality of the created product. On the other hand – and this suggests one aspect of the paradox – this new kind can only appear as exemplified in singular, individual, unique products. Creative acts lead to results which, as identities in difference, are general as examples of their kind, while, at the same time, they are uniquely different.

Another side of this paradox can be seen if we consider further the relation of new and thus unfamiliar kinds to their exemplifications or instantiations in the world. Creative acts seem to issue in the appearances in time of timeless identities that are knowable apart from their specific, temporal occurrences in the world. Although such new Forms are intelligible, because of their unfamiliarity, they seem to have no basis for intelligibility in anything except themselves. This puzzle is not simply the puzzle that faces any theory that tries to account for the relationship between atemporal identities, or what might be thought of as Platonic Ideas, and the particulars that exemplify them. In the case of new identities, the puzzle is intensified. A complex that is new is disclosed in an intimacy with the concrete specificity of the object in which it initially occurs. Such specifity is disregarded and, indeed, is irrelevant when we consider familiar identities. In the case of what is familiar, intelligibility is present when an identity is discerned, regardless of the contingencies of its instantiation.

The paradox of creation also can be seen in the activity of the creative artist. It is important to consider how the paradox is seen here, because persons interested in art, and artists themselves often insist that past traditions, styles, and personal experiences influence and condition what the artist produces. (Similarly, scientific concepts seem to condition scientific creation.) Thus, the continuities that do hold between acts of creation and their antecedents are emphasized and made the subject of fascination. I do not deny such continuities. But I do contend that exclusive emphasis on them overlooks equally evident features of the art process – features that are even more important than continuities, since it is these which alert us to the possibility that the process is creative rather than repetitive of established continuities. The artist begins a creative process without a preconceived plan or concept of the exact complex of qualities in the object which he will create. If he were to start with such a plan, then creation already would be complete in his mind. But the creator does begin with a certain talent and set of established habits of work. At first, he senses that certain elements are required in the future product, but he does not yet know these are. And as he creates, he somehow discovers what he wants to create. He formulates his plan at the same time that he comes to see what that plan is – at the same time that he sees what is required to complete the process he started. Paradoxically, then, the creator must at once create and discover. He must generate a necessitated product which is not necessitated by anything given to the creator with which he can generate it. In short, the creator must act as an agent which is a cause without a prior cause, a cause which causes itself.

At first glance, it might seem that the puzzles or paradoxes of creativity bear out the claims of those who insist on mystery. However, I do not believe the issue can be so easily settled. The rationalist as well as the non-rationalist may agree that (from the standpoint of the human creator) instances of creativity do seem to be paradoxical. The appearance in the world of new intelligible kinds is not something denied by either the advocate of mystery or the advocate of a rationalistic interpretation of creativity. Both traditions acknowledge that in some sense unexpected and unpredicted identities appear. This is accepted as a primary datum of experience. The issue between the two traditions, however, centers on how the appearance is to be interpreted. On the one hand, if we say that what appears is only surprising, that if we had time and knowledge, it could be exhaustively subjected to conceptual understanding, then we interpret the creative act as the rationalists do. On the other hand, if we say that the phenomenon cannot be brought under a rational explanation, if we say that the discontinuities that precede appearances of newness are unintelligible and not understandable, then we take the side of those who appeal to the presence of mystery in the world. And if we follow the dominant strand of this tradition, we look for the source of creativity in a power, though a power fundamentally mysterious, that transcends human activity.

As I have said earlier, it seems to me that both of these interpretations are misdirected. I can now indicate further the basis for this claim. Both views are misdirected because they both turn away from the phenomenon with which they start, that is, the apppearance of novelty. They both refuse to acknowledge what is crucial in the initial appearance of novelty and the inescapability of the paradox in this appearance. In the first place, we should notice that the rationalist's view of creativity cannot be proven, either by scientific verification or by conclusive demonstration. The best the rationalist can do is hope that in the future explanations will be found. This hope, of course, is not a proof. We can only wait and see. But if the rationalistic perspective cannot be proven, then it must be offered as a recommendation for interpreting creative acts. It is a recommendation, a demand of reason, to regard creative acts as events in a continuum of regularities or lawful process. To regard them in this way is to treat them as not being what they also appear to be – occurrences of unfamiliar identities that are intelligible even though they are not continuous with their antecedents.

But the contrary view cannot be proven either. Its proponents can argue that the rationalist view is dubious and that the denial that explanation of creativity is possible is a plausible thesis, since it conforms to the peculiarities of certain kinds of phenomena. Thus, it can claim to be a view that remains closer to the phenomenon of creativity than does the rationalist position, for the demand for a rationalistic explanation simply ignores the mysterious aspect of creative activity. However, in the final analysis, the view that affirms mystery in the creativity of an ultimate and transcendent source also strays from the phenomenon. The sense in which it strays can be seen if we emphasize the ways a super-human source must be viewed as a foundation for creativity.

Tracing the creative act to a transcendent source may be carried out in either of two ways. As already suggested, one strand in the rationalist tradition may claim what initially appears as a mystery may be understood in terms of a source which is independent of finite consciousness but which itself is non-mysterious or intelligible. This source may be regarded as an omniscient and omnipotent God. Or, it may be a non-divine source, perhaps an individual unconscious or a generalized unconscious, or a life force.[8] Even though this approach introduces notions not bound directly by experimental data and observable behavior, it does take the form of a rationalism, since it treats creative acts as understandable within continuities flowing from the transcendent source. The paradox of human creations is treated as an appearance rather than a reality. The mystery is only an illusion for those who are ignorant of the *logos* of the ultimate source.

[8] It would be misleading to suggest that every view that appeals to such sources is non-naturalistic. Freud's appeal to the individual unconscious, for instance, is ordinarily thought to fall under naturalism. However, a non-naturalistic view (at least in contrast to a naturalism that requires a rigorous system and a dependence on natural science) may refer creativity to a specific source which serves as explanatory. Such a view is rationalistic at bottom and is opposed to those which affirm ultimate mystery.

The other version of supernaturalism also appeals to a super-human source. But, unlike the rationalist view, it re-affirms the mystery within the source. On this alternative, paradox remains. Yet its locus is placed outside of the phenomenon in which it initially appeared.

Now, in all of these alternatives – that is, in the view that assumes the possibility of naturalistic explanation, in the non-naturalistic but rationalist view that traces creativity to an intelligible source transcendent of finite conscious aspects, and in the view that sees the transcendent source as ultimately mysterious – in all of these, the responsibility and origination of creativity in the finite agent is denied. The view that the artist is autonomous and responsible – is a conscious agent acting from his own resources – is rejected. For the rationalists, the paradox and mystery are considered a function of ignorance, and the creator is seen as a conditioned consequent. For the non-rationalist, the paradox of the origin of novelty is affirmed but excluded from the finite act in which we initially encounter it as an appearance, and novelty is thought to have its origin elsewhere. On either of these alternatives, the finite agent is not responsible for the novelty it appears to originate. The naturalist, the rationalist, and the non-rationalist fail to acknowledge the finite agent as a source which can originate newness of kind.

We are faced with two alternatives. On the one hand, we can choose to deny that finite creative acts are essentially paradoxical by adopting views which cannot be proven and which, I shall argue later, are themselves in danger of admitting other paradoxes. On the other hand, we can choose to admit that finite agents can themselves be sources of creativity and that these sources are essentially paradoxical and thus in a sense unintelligible from the standpoint of our traditional ways of understanding. I choose the second alternative. This choice points to an alliance with non-rationalism. But this alliance is limited, for the choice I make is to admit that what appears to be paradoxical has its locus within the creator's own activity. The argument in favor of this choice will be developed in the second chapter of this book. In brief, it depends upon two considerations. First, to admit that finite acts of creation are essentially paradoxical is to face the paradox where it is initially presented – in the appearances of the origin of novelty within finite activities. It is in such phenomena that we find the originator responsible for creations. Thus we call the artist the creator, albeit the discoverer too, of his creation. The spontaneity we find and the responsibility we attribute to an agent in creative activities appears in the finite activities of the agent. The second consideration which leads me to reject the rationalist and non-rationalist tradition is that these are no better off in the final analysis than the view I hold, for both lead to their own puzzles and paradoxes, as I shall try to show in later discussions.

In choosing to face spontaneity and paradox in finite acts, I do not think it follows that creative acts are in every sense incapable of being understood. What is required is another, a third approach to creativity, an approach which presupposes a kind of understanding different in aim from the kind of conceptual understanding according to which creativity appears paradoxical. Such an approach must maintain an openness to paradox. This openness must be more than a willingness to admit that something in the world is incomprehensible. Rather, it must be a fundamental philosophical orientation on our part. It must be a willingness not merely to agree that there are some things in the world that cannot be explained, but it must abandon certain aspects of the purpose of understanding which is presupposed by the traditional approaches. Further, it must be a willingness to accept the appearance of irreducible paradox for what it is. It must be an openness to the immediate experience of paradox, an experience in which we do not reason or deliberate, but an experience of directly responding to, and (in a sense) understanding, what is paradoxical.

As a final indication of the view I shall offer in the succeeding chapters, let me pursue the point about being open to the paradoxical. The irreducibly paradoxical, I think, appears in every creative act and in every response of an observer whose attention is controlled by this act. The paradoxical appearance of unprecedented Form, of the creative agent as a self-causing cause, must be accepted in its own terms, without recourse to a hoped-for principle of explanation or a source beyond the appearance. The response I am suggesting, however, is not one that need occur only on very rare occasions. I believe that we encounter the paradox of creativity more often than we might realize. We experience it in every aesthetic response to a work of art that is a creation.

In responding to a work of art in its own terms, the observer's attention focuses directly and immediately on an emerging or developing complex or identity that appears for him in much the same way that newness of kind appears for the creator. The new identity is gradually identified within the limits of an evolving, temporal experience. The complex seems to emerge; it appears as a changing structure. Thus, a general necessity seems to require that the elements of the work relate to one another in specific ways. But this necessity, which requires these relations, changes as the aesthetic experience develops. Thus, on the one hand, there seems to be a strict necessity, but, on the other hand, this necessity changes as the art work varies from moment to moment in the aesthetic experience. For example, consider the introductory passage of a musical composition such as Beethoven's Fifth Symphony. What this passage "means" (the musical sense it has for us) when initially heard changes after we have heard more of the composition. The persistent rhythm established by the introduction affects the entire first movement, and in doing so, it affects the way the introduction must be understood in the context of the whole movement. Meanings interact and affect one another. No element is understood without an understanding of the other elements – ideally, all of them – and, in turn, all these elements must be understood with reference to the complete complex of interrelations that necessitate them.

Another way to put this is to say that in aesthetic appreciation, we experience something that appears to us as a structure that is at once complete and incomplete. It is complete in the sense that it appears as a requirement and as a governing necessity for each constituent in the work of art as we pass from one element to another. Yet the structure is incomplete in the sense that we cannot identify it until all elements cohere in a unity that comprises the entire work of art. The elements interrelated must be apprehended before we can know the structure of the work. The structure and the relation of the elements are one – together they constitute the created object.

The point is that, although we are not responsible in the way the artist is, the new identity in a work of art comes into being for the observer in much the same way that it must come into being for the creator. Like the creator, we, the observers, do not know what is required in the work until it is complete for our attention. At the same time, we can only understand each moment or each element of the work in terms of a dimly known structure that requires each of the elements.

The work of art presents us with paradox. Yet in aesthetic experience, this paradox is acceptable. We "understand" it just to the extent that we understand and make sense of the work of art. There is no need to find something external to the work of art to make it meaningful to us while we encounter it in the immediacy of aesthetic experience. The paradoxical appearance is not baffling for aesthetic attention. It simply is given. Only when we reflect and try to understand the work from *outside,* do we demand that the paradox either be resolved or be traced to an ultimate source.

What I am recommending, then, is that an adequate approach to creativity be based on a model of understanding akin to the understanding of the aesthetic appreciator. And if this approach is taken, paradox can be accepted as given. Thus, a theory of creativity ought to accept paradox where it is immediately found. And a theory which thus accepts paradox and tries to include creativity can permit the individual agent of each creative act to be the source (though a paradoxical source) of this act.

Although the model of understanding that I have suggested shares common ground with understanding in aesthetic experience, it includes more than aesthetic experience. There are crucial features of the traditional model of understanding that provide a framework for knowledge of creativity. The identification and role of these features will be part of the discussion to follow.

In the following chapters, I shall take up the issues raised by my claims that the two opposed traditions are inadequate to the phenomenon of creativity. My purpose will be to explore the possibility of articulating a conceptual framework for understanding creativity which is open to radically creative acts.

Although the discussion will concern novelty in general, creativity in the art process will serve as a model and point of departure. If the general features of situations in which novelty occurs are, by virtue of their generality, common to all instances of novelty, then an analysis which looks to creativity in art as a model ought to disclose those general features; and it should do so more clearly and more emphatically than analyses of other processes, since the production of novelty seems to be exhibited most obviously in art processes. Indeed, novelty as we ordinarily are interested in it is displayed in art (or at least "great" art) almost as a paradigm; for it shows itself as that which is the "freshness," the "originality," the "created character," of objects that sustain the evidence of creativity – that is, that persist in appearing original and which do not become stereotyped or "old hat." Further, to study spontaneity in art should not do violence to the differences between creativity there and in other fields of endeavor, or even between human action and natural process. For no claim need be made that all the characteristics of the art process are common to other kinds of creative activity. The analysis of art need only seek the aspects of novelty that reveal its relation to the origin of novelty, independently of nuances and variations in its appearance elsewhere.

The first chapter will be devoted to a discussion of what is meant by creativity in the radical sense. As already suggested, what is needed is more attention than is ordinarily given to characterizing creativity. Thus, I shall elaborate the concept of "newness of kind" which points to the paradoxical character of creative acts.

The second chapter will examine the paradox of creativity. I shall describe the paradox by pointing out how certain inevitable difficulties face the inquirer who seeks to understand the origination of novelty. I shall then develop an argument for affirming that creativity is a kind of radical activity that reveals discontinuity in the world as it exhibits novelty. In short, I shall offer reasons for holding the view that creativity is "arational."

In the third chapter, I shall propose a thesis about the extent to which novelty can be made intelligible. I shall pursue the suggestion that aesthetic experience provides a crucial part of the model that is most adequate to understanding the origin of novelty. Metaphorical expressions will be examined in order to make this point. Thus, it will be argued that although spontaneity cannot be fully understood in terms of traditional rational principles, it can be understood in terms of an approach that takes metaphorical expression as its model.

The fourth chapter will continue the consideration of the intelligibility of novelty in relation to other models of understanding. It is here that I shall try to show how full understanding of creativity must include more than is present in the model drawn from aesthetic experience.

CHAPTER I

PRODUCTION AND RADICAL CREATION

INTRODUCTION

Every attempt to understand something presupposes a concept of what is to be understood. However, few studies of creativity include careful and critical consideration of the characteristics of acts that are thought to be creative. These characteristics are assumed. And they serve a role, usually tacit, in determining the direction inquiry takes. Generally, neither the assumptions nor the role the assumed characteristics play in determining the direction of inquiry have been examined carefully.

The following discourse, then, must begin with an attempt to single out the features of creative acts that seem necessary for those acts to be regarded as creative. I do not propose to define creativity, if definition is taken to be rigorous and analytic. But I do intend to bring into focus the key characteristics expected of created achievement. Thus, the characterization I shall offer is at once descriptive and normative. I shall identify features which I claim are properly relevant to characterizing created objects and which ought to be included in a characterization of creativity. Although there is a recommendation offered, the characterization is not simply a stipulation. It is based on a description of what I think we observe coupled with a discrimination of what permits us to distinguish some objects as creations from others that are not creations. Let me emphasize that the main focus of this chapter will be to offer a description of phenomena insofar as they seem to manifest themselves as created. Such a description must precede arguments intended to show why we are not deluded about what appears. In the next chapter, I shall consider this possibility as well as the problem of explaining what is described.

The first step in characterizing creative acts will be to suggest a way of identifying "novelty" or "newness." I take it for granted that characterizing an activity depends upon distinguishing its product from products of other activities. Thus, I shall first ask about the generic characteristics of the kind of products that are regarded as created. In turn I shall consider the features of the kind of acts that lead to such products. In identifying general features that distinguish an object as new, I shall not be concerned initially with whether the newness of the object guarantees that the object is the product of a creative act. However, my final aim is to characterize not routine acts of making or repetitive achievements, but rather those more profound and dramatic productive processes associated with genius and thought of as examples of what we call "originality" or, sometimes, the "genuinely creative." As suggested in the Introduction, it seems strategically advantageous to approach creativity where it is most clearly evident. It is the more prominent and dramatic cases of creativity that have attracted inquiry, and presumably an understanding of these will throw light on the less dramatic cases.

After the general qualifications of newness have been identified, I shall consider what it is to be created as well as new. In order to do this, it will be necessary to introduce and to examine briefly what is meant by the concept of "Form." Against this background, I shall discuss various qualifications required to identify a process as creative as well as one that issues in something new. I shall contend that an act that is creative must, in a special way, be controlled and must yield a product which is valuable and new with respect to its structure and Form. The suggestion about the requirement of value will be explored briefly in order to indicate one of the directions a complete study of creativity must take.

A. NOVELTY PROPER

1. *Individuality and Radical Newness*

It will be assumed at the outset that anyone who has expressed an interest in creativity acknowledges that some phenomena at least seem to be new. There are occasions when things, whether they be events, objects, qualities, or categories, appear in certain respects (though not in every respect) to be disconnected or dissociated from what went before them. The question of whether or not appearances of newness are real or only illusory will be discussed later. At this stage of the discussion, it is claimed simply that sometimes things *seem* to us to be different from the past. On such occasions, what occurs appears to be unprecedented – or, more strongly, unpredictable – in the light of what was known before it was encountered. Such phenomena are not reducible to what was known before they occurred. Even if one were to insist that this unprecedentedness or irreducibility could be proven to be illusory, and even if the phenomenon could later be shown by causal explanation to have been predictable, the possibility of such proof and explanation is distinct from the observation that some phenomena appear to be unpredictable.

Initially, then, I shall consider what is, without theoretical interpretation, regarded as the newness of created objects. Accordingly, I shall provisionally maintain neutrality with respect to explaining newness. In other words, I shall at present assume only what may be thought of as the phenomenological objectivity of the appearance of newness and inquire into its relevance for creative acts.[1]

On the basis of the observation that some phenomena appear to be new in the way I have suggested, it seems that a necessary condition of novelty is the presence in an object of irreducible and unprecedented or unpredictable difference. However, it is obvious that if novelty were nothing more than irreducible, unprecedented difference between an individual thing and its antecedents, then novelty could be ascribed to every discriminable thing. Each event or object in the world can be considered new with respect to its singularity. For example, no matter how much one penny may be like another of the same stamp, the first can be thought of as a particular object which occupies a different spatial location and, if inspected closely, must vary ever so slightly from the other penny. Similarly, the penny is different from all other things, including its antecedents. It is dissociated from all other things in time precisely to the extent that it is distinguishable from all other particulars. Even spatial and temporal conditions, apart from the specific properties of things, can distinguish particulars in the sense of difference at issue here. In this sense, all things are different, or numerically novel as particular individuals, that is, all things instance novelty of singularity.[2]

---

[1] It should be obvious that my intention is to avoid facing at this stage the metaphysical issue of determinism and indeterminism broached in the Introduction. Some form of determinism lies behind the claim that what appears to be unprecedented is an occurrence which is only surprising and which is, in the final analysis, explicable and traceable to antecedents. This isuue will be central to the next chapter.

[2] It may be remarked in passing that novelty of singularity seems to be the kind of newness admissible and emphasized by one side of a Whiteheadian treatment of creativity as it is exemplified in human activity. Thus newness is ascribable to the uniqueness of every event or actual entity. I shall indicate certain limitations in a Whiteheadian approach to creativity in the next chapter. It should be pointed out here that for the sake of precision, a distinction may be made between singulars and particulars, or between singularity and particularity. A singular is an individual having its identity independently of anything else. Its identity as an individual is not known by reference to its being a member of a class or an instance of a universal or set of universals. By contrast, a particular is an individual having its identity as one among other particulars.

Some things, however, appear to be novel in another, more radical way. Radical novelty appears on those occasions in which there is difference not only of singularity, but also of structure and Form – or of what for the moment I shall refer to as difference of kind. Let me develop this point by considering how singular things can be said to be intelligible and how they manifest uniqueness.[3] Let us consider what it is about two pencils that makes them intelligible to us. The first and most simple question we can ask about them is, What are they? It is significant that we have taken a step toward answering this question in having referred to them by the same term. We have indicated that they are two distinct objects to which the same name is applied. Because of this, we have initially identified them. But this identification is not merely an act of naming. It is grounded on an identity. The identity need not be an essence or actual unitary closed set of properties. It may be "loose" and "open," extending to borderline cases. But ideally the identity serves as a controlling focus for recognition and attribution of a name and for predication. What more, then, can be said about this identity and thus about the answer to the question, What are they? We see that they are yellow, cylindrical, or more precisely they are hexagonal; they have certain dimensions. Each has a brass band at one end that encloses an eraser, and each has a lead core. Finally, they are recognized as things that can perform a specific function, that of writing.

Though it is a singular, its identity as a particular thing is known by reference to the kind, or the class, to which it belongs. A particular is known as a particular thing in a group, all of which are instances of a universal or set of universals.

[3] I should point out before continuing further that I use the word "intelligible" in a broad sense to refer to the possibility of being a recognizable specific determination. An object is intelligible if it is at least identifiable and characterizable. For purposes to be indicated later in this chapter as well as in other discussion in this book, I hold the view that there are occasions of immediate, non-discursive cognition. Thus, in some instances, an individual may be intelligible by virtue of a unique determination which is an object for cognition, but which is not, in the moment of cognition, relatable to other known objects. The possibility of immediate, non-discursive knowledge is essential to any view which acknowledges that new intelligibility can occur for human knowledge. I think it is also essential to any view that interprets intelligibility as dependent upon identity discerned within differences. (I do not intend to say that those individuals which are thus immediately intelligible are therefore fully intelligible. Indeed, I shall argue later that there is an element of unintelligibility in them. Nor do I claim that every individual is intelligible as unique, but only that there are some occasions in which the uniqueness of an individual is intelligible.) In one sense, Duns Scotus' principle of Heccaeity is suggestive of the view I am proposing, for this principle calls for the possibility of a "contracted" form that gives intelligibility to an individual. On the other hand, C. S. Peirce's category of Secondness, as what resists intelligibility in the individuality of things, points to my claim that something unintelligible is present in individuals. At the same time, however, Peirce also acknowledges the point I am suggesting, because he speaks of the possibility that cognition terminates in a system which consists in a unified structure of thought known by a final, "true opinion." Here, the object, reality, is a unique determination (an individual) for "true opinion." This point, of course, is arguable and I am perfectly aware that I am suggesting only one interpretation of one side of Peirce's philosophy.

We should observe that with respect to the characteristics by which we identify the pencils, they are the same, although there are two pencils rather than a single object. In saying what they are, we have not distinguished them from each other. As I shall point out in a moment, if we look more closely, we can see that minute differences are evident. One pencil has a rough place on the side of the eraser. The other has a faded spot on the printing along the side. Each is in its own spatial location, and each can be used in different contexts – in different places by different people for different specific writing purposes.

Now, what does the answer given thus far to the question, "What are these objects?" show us about our knowledge of the pencils? In identifying them, we have taken a step toward knowing or understanding them. In answering the question, "What are they?" we have taken a step toward making them intelligible. First of all, the common name they bear indicates something about them that is at least a condition for their being known. The name is a sign for things that exhibit a cluster of characteristics ascribed to both objects. And it is this cluster of characteristics that enables us to know what the objects are. The cluster of characteristics is a condition of the intelligibility of the objects.[4]

To say that identified interconnected characteristics make a thing intelligible is not to say that some characteristics are essential while others are accidental and that only the essential characteristics are the condition of intelligibility. All of the characteristics may contribute to what can in various degrees and ways be known about the pencils. However, in the case of the pencils, some characteristics are more relevant than others with respect to our current understanding of these objects as instances among other instances of things known.[5] Most relevant for these objects is their shape and the quality of the lead in the center, less relevant are the minute variations, such as the rough place on the eraser, least relevant is the color, etc. These are dissociated from the identity of the cluster of characteristics by which the objects are understood to be pencils. Such differences do not

---

[4] In order not to avoid at least acknowledging a problem, I should admit here a distinction between a thing taken in its totality and what it is in its intelligibility. I do not insist that the characteristics that show the intelligibility of the thing exhaust that thing. Whether by matter, or some other principle of individuation, there is something more. There is a "core" or focus to the thing, and this focus is neither identical with nor fully explicable in terms of the totality of qualities which are associated with the thing.

[5] The point here is that a rigid essentialism need not be adopted. Intelligibility depends upon coherence of clusterings of characteristics, and the coherence may be broad, loose, and vague, though ideally it must be philosophically grounded on a focus of unification. The importance of this point in the light of Wittgenstein's attack on essentialism will be seen in Chapter III.

contribute to or detract from the identity of the pencils, insofar as we understand what they are. Because some characteristics are more relevant to one another such that the cluster is intelligible, each cluster of characteristics may be called a "complex," a grouping that has an order by virtue of which it is coherent and thus intelligible.

Let us next consider two objects of a different kind, e.g., paintings, one by Cézanne and the other by Klee. Again, let us ask, "What are they?" As in the case of the pencils, the first answer to this question may consist in identifying them. They are identified generally as works of art and more specifically as paintings. But these objects at once demand that we can or ought to be more precise. First of all, they have been given titles, and they are discriminated as the products of certain artists. One is by Klee and is called "The Red Bridge." The other is by Cézanne and is called "Large Pine in Red Soil." Each can be identified in terms of a style, and as belonging to a tradition in painting: German expressionism, in the case of the Klee, and Post-Impressionism, in the case of the Cézanne. Further, the characteristics that contribute to the identity of each can be discriminated with further exactness. Quite fine discriminations can be made, and these discriminations are relevant to our saying what each object is. Indeed, these discriminations are crucial to the identities of the paintings. They determine not only the tradition, style, and painter by which the objects are identified, but also the specific identification of this work of the painter in contrast to other works by the same painter. Such specific identification makes reference to such features as brush strokes, colors and color relationships, ways of varying representational elements, etc.

The extent to which relatively minute differences of quality bear on the identities of the paintings reveals a difference between the intelligibility of these objects and the intelligibility of the pencils. Minute and subtle characteristics are more relevant here than in the case of the pencils. The qualities of each of the paintings are so interwoven that they constitute something that is virtually a world of its own. Each painting, of course, has relations to other objects, including things that are not paintings and that are not works of art. They bear relations to these pencils, for example, just as these pencils are related to other objects. But each painting, at the same time, exhibits specific differences in its features so exactly and with such interdependence that the paintings are identifiable by their internal constitutions.[6] The complex of characteristics that are thus internally re-

---

[6] The integration of all aspects of a painting in constituting its intelligibility is a widely acknowledged condition of meaning in art. A number of writers have defended

lated function in a way similar to an organic system, constituting these objects as what they are (as having their own identities). In this way they are autonomous.

But can we not say that the pencils too have an internal constitution? They are made of wood that has specific properties. For example, each has the property of being sufficiently hard to hold the lead but sufficiently soft to enable us to sharpen the pencil. Also, the lead is of a certain degree of hardness, has a certain consistency, and is placed in a definite relationship to the wood that surrounds it. We could pursue an analysis of the pencils, moving to deeper (or higher) levels of penetration. We could turn to a scientific (physical-chemical) analysis in terms of molecular and atomic structure. But the point that the pencils have certain internal constitutions is, I think, obvious.

Does this point imply that the pencils are like the works of art in being autonomous and in being constituted as worlds of their own? I think not, at least not in the sense that the paintings are composed of interdependent components. The internal constitutions of the pencils are identities that are common to both pencils and to pencils of all kinds, just insofar as the elements of the pencils are ordered in accord with their conventional contexts and established uses – namely, specific kinds of writing instruments. Their intelligibility is a function of their identities as a single kind of thing designed for a defined purpose. By contrast, the intelligibility of each painting lies not only in its identity as a painting, its being an instance of a tradition and of a style, or its being an instance of a work of art, etc., but the identity of each painting and thus its intelligibility is singular or individualized. The cluster of characteristics that constitute what the paintings are constitutes them both as things belonging to the same kind and as things that exhibit a unique "kind," an unprecedented type. Each is a kind of its own, and what it is in its distinctive organization does not depend on a preconceived general purpose for which it is designed. Its boundaries mark off a domain that can in a sense be entered, explored, and that controls our understanding of it, not only because of its boundaries, but also because of a central focus or concentration around which the characteristics in the work cluster.

It is probably obvious that one of the points that can be seen in this

---

this acknowledgement. Dewey, in *Art as Experience* (New York: Minton, Balch & Company, 1934), is perhaps the best known writer in American aesthetic theory to have vigorously argued for the description of organic-like organization in art. In any case, Dewey's position is significant because he affirms so well some of the same characteristics of created objects that I do, while he overlooks a crucial feature of meaning and intelligibility in created objects – the paradoxical aspect of this intelligibility.

consideration of the difference between the works of art and the pencils is that works of art can serve as models of objects distinguished as novel in a radical sense. Both pencils and works of art are products of certain processes. But pencils and works of art differ with respect to the way they are intelligible. Pencils are products that belong to one kind, of which there are other equally good examples already produced and identified. Works of art are products each of which presents its own kind, and for each of which there are no other examples. There is no other example of this work, "The Red Bridge" by Paul Klee.[7] The way in which works of art are exclusive examples and thus models will be viewed more closely in later chapters. At this stage of the discussion, however, I am primarily concerned with indicating what I think is meant (or *ought* to be meant) by the novelty of objects that are new in a more radical sense than numerical novelty.

What I have tried to show in the discussion of the paintings and the pencils is that the subtleties that are exhibited by a singular thing may contribute to that thing in a special way. In such cases, the cluster of characteristics by which the thing is known is a unique "Gestalt," an identity not known before the occurrence of the thing. This identity as it is exhibited in a concrete object is what I shall refer to as a structure.[8]

---

[7] There are, of course, problems raised by my claim here. One might ask about reproductions of the so-called same painting. One might ask whether or not I must treat the work of art as something that is not completely restricted to being a single physical object hanging in an art gallery. And one might ask whether the singularity of a poem or a musical composition is not basically different from that of a painting. These are questions that I must waive at the moment. Yet it is necessary to nod in their direction. I think that if one takes an empirical or a physicalist interpretation of works of art, or of aesthetic objects in general, what I have said about the uniqueness of kind of a work of art holds just as well on this interpretation as it does for an idealistic view of aesthetic objects — or, closer to my own interpretation, for a kind of Platonic realism applied to aesthetic objects. It is true, however, that what I have said about the uniqueness of kind of works of art leads to a particular interpretation of the ontological status of works of art, and consideration of the place of works of art in an ontology of creativity must be postponed.

[8] It should be noted that in this discussion a structure is something like a form in the sense of an Aristotelean interpretation of form as immanent. Thus a form is conceived as a participant within particular things. As such, a structure is an ordered composite of properties which appear as a particular and which appear to be relevant to one another because of an identity or a determinateness of focus that is the basis for their mutual relevance. However, because the determinateness or identity is an indispensable condition for the intelligibility of the structure, the identity has a status which is for cognition distinct with respect to temporal changes in the qualities of the particular. It is by virtue of the identity which makes the particular intelligible that the structure is recognized. The identity of a structure, then, is like a Platonic form which serves to render particulars knowable. Such an identity is what I shall call "Form," and sometimes "matrix" or "pattern." These terms as I use them suggest that the status of what I refer to is distinct from physical and mental location. That which is physical or mental is changing and ambiguous so long as a distinguishable identity (a Form) is not discerned to make it intelligible. Thus, a particular that appears as having a new structure

Insofar as a structure is distinctive, individual, and unique, this structure is unfamiliar in the sense that it is different from all other structures. It is, therefore, unlike the kind of structure that enables us to bring the two pencils under the single concept of "pencil." Further, insofar as this different structure came into existence at some time, it was then new. Thereafter it can be seen as new with respect to the past that is related to its initial occurrence. This point, of course, is important to the task of characterizing created character. It also calls attention to why it is tempting to think of creations as new in the sense of numerical novelty. Newness of kind is a newness of what is singular. But the singularity here is not sheer difference, or a condition for being singled out as one and only one thing. The singularity of newness of kind is singularity of intelligibility – intelligibility of a discernibly coherent complex.

Before pursuing the relation of the concept of new structure to the characterization of created character, it is necessary to say something more about the status of structures, that is, about the way they make objects intelligible. A structure is an ordering of concrete items, each of which can be abstractly regarded as a unit. In the case of works of art, these units are ordered with reference to one another and to the togetherness, or to the ordering that connects them. They do not add up to make a collection of independently known items. In short, the components or units of a work of art are ordered in a way that is very much like an organic unity. This point will be discussed at greater length later. What is important here is to emphasize that when a structure is new in being different from every other structure, its structured components must (at least when initially identified) function together much like the components of an organism. The uniqueness of kind, the identity of an individual in its individuality, requires an intimacy within the complex that other complexes, such as those that constitute pencils, do not require. The connections among the properties of one pencil are common to the connections in another pencil. They share something – the order of their structures. By contrast, in instances of new structures, as illustrated by the works of art, the way in which connections provide the identity and thus the intelligibility of each such structure must be unique. Consequently, new structures depend upon the special roles of their constituents, a kind of role not played in other instances.

One consequence of this special feature of new structures is that such structures are intimately bound to the determinate objects that they consti-

---

appears so by virtue of somehow newly exemplifying a Form. My interpretation of Form will be discussed further below.

tute.[9] Although they are not, as new, common to a range of particulars (they are not generals), they appear to intelligence as "embedded," as given all their specificity in determinate objects. They are wedded to individuals, and in that sense they are concrete. Human intelligence seems to require recognition of the individual object in order to discern the new intelligibility, for it is in such concreteness that the components are uniquely ordered.

At the same time, however, the structure cannot be wholly bound by the concrete object. It must endure in order to be identified. The new structure, while unprecedented and dependent upon individuality, is after all an identity. But if it is an identity, it is not wholly dependent on what it identifies. Nor is the structure wholly atemporal and independent of its concrete presence in time. Thus it is not strictly identical with its intelligibility. It is not (not quite) an Idea or form, even in some loose Platonic sense. It and the object which it makes intelligible endure; yet it shares with its constituents whatever mutability they have. On the other hand, since it endures, it manifests something that is not time-bound; it resists differentiations in moments of time. It cannot be exhausted in any one moment or in the series of moments that comprise the period of time when it is recognized. It manifests something immutable. Again, if it did not, it could not be sustained as an identity. Indeed, it could not have endured at all if it did not show resistance to temporality. The something it shows, I call Form. And the way it shows a Form, is by exemplifying it.

Now, if the discussion thus far is to provide a step toward characterizing created character, it is important to see that the uniqueness of a singular may exhibit a structure which, in turn, exemplifies a Form different from all Forms with respect to which other singular things or particulars previously had been classified as particulars. The Form of a new structure could not be an intelligible identity by which the particular exhibiting the structure was antecedently recognized. Thus, uniqueness is constituted in the difference of structure and is known in the difference of the Form of the singular in question. With respect to the different Form, the thing is determined by an intelligible identity not discernible within established knowledge. Novelty of the more radical kind, then, is identifiable in instances whose determinateness consists in a special order or organization

[9] They are, to repeat, the sorts of things that might be thought of in one respect as Aristotelean forms. But the immanence of such structures is appropriate to so-called immaterial as well as material objects. A new idea has a structure exhibited in an ordered medium of expression. The immateriality of the idea transcends this structure – this point will be treated in the context of structures of such objects as paintings and pencils in a moment – but the idea is first instanced in a structure, whether it be in spoken and written speech or in determinate objects of thought.

of the new thing. Let us call this more radical novelty, "Novelty Proper." [10] An object that has Novelty Proper instances a different structure and Form. It *exhibits* a new structure which newly *exemplifies* a Form.

Instances of Novelty Proper necessarily vary with respect to the kinds of processes from which they issue. For example, the structure of a musical composition is different from that of a painting in the differences in concrete elements that compose their structures. The structure of a new moral ideal differs from that of a new work of art. However, all instances share in the character of being the appearance of a structure that exemplifies a Form which is different from all prior instances of exemplified Forms. I shall mention only a few illustrations. Novelty Proper is present in first occurrences of plant or animal species in biological evolution. The differences between an old and "new" species are sufficiently radical and impressive for them to be discriminated as new kinds of life. In citing the evolution of kinds as exemplifying Novelty Proper, I am, of course, assuming that a new kind or species is a new instancing of a Form. And this assumption depends upon the insistence that what is identifiable as a kind is descried – that is, identified for the first time – by virtue of a Form or definite identity.

Other examples can be found in the history of art. Any work which manifests a different style within a tradition, such as that of Renoir within

---

[10] The term "novelty proper," has been used before by Gustav Bergmann in a way similar to though not identical with the way I use it: "Holism, Historicism, and Emergence," *Philosophy of Science*, Vol. II, No. 4 (October, 1944), p. 210 ff. However, Bergmann's view of what can be understood about such novelty differs from mine. This diference should be evident in the next chapter. The introduction of the term "Novelty Proper" was suggested to me by R. G. Collingwood's term "art proper" which distinguishes what is correctly from what is falsely called "art" (*The Principles of Art* [Oxford: Clarendon Press, 1938], in particular, Chapter III). Thus "Novelty Proper" is used to refer to a kind of novelty that is less pervasive and more appropriately called "novelty" than the newness shared by all individuals. The term is normative insofar as the word "proper" suggests how "novelty" ought to be applied. C. Lloyd Morgan's "primary novelty" comes close to the meaning I wish to suggest. See *The Emergence of Novelty* (London: Kegan Paul & Company, 1933). Morgan's "primary novelty" refers to initial occurrences of unprecedented complexes or relations and is intended to distinguish between what "emerges" for the first time and emergents that are repetitions of what was novel in the past. The question whether novelty "emerges," comes from causes which are in principle knowable, or simply pops into the world spontaneously, is, as already indicated, waived for the moment. A penetrating discussion of the concept of emergence and the appearance of novelty is to be found in Paul Henle's "The Status of Emergence," *The Journal of Philosophy* XXXIX, No. 18 (August 27, 1942), pp. 486-493. Henle also conceives of novelty as very much like my "Novelty Proper." It may be observed here, too, that the notion of "Novelty Proper" should mark the common ground between my characterization of newness and one side of a Whiteheadian view. An eternal object which is exemplified for the first time would indeed appear as an instance of Novelty Proper. However, if an eternal object can be new for human knowledge and for the actual world, then some processes must be new in a more radical sense than that attributable to the uniqueness of every process.

Impressionism, exemplifies a Form different from the Form with respect to which it is a particular art work, that is, a Form different from previous Forms of art works that constitute the tradition of Impressionism. Or an individual painting may exhibit a coherent structure which exemplifies a different Form with respect to a style peculiar to the painter. Thus, in the production of art, Novelty Proper may occur in an object whose Form serves to initiate a tradition or a style within a tradition; or it may occur in an object whose Form is a variation within a style.

Novelty Proper, then, appears with the first exemplification of a Form. Thereafter, the new thing may be regarded as new provided that we see the contrast between its structure and Form and the structures and Forms that had been apprehended before its first occurrence.

Yet it might be asked, How can one justify describing the newness appropriate to created objects in such a way as to generate puzzles? Why propose a thesis which is defined so that an ineradicable problem is confronted? Most simply, the answer I must give is that I have characterized newness in accord with what I believe we find when we look at things that are often thought of as creations when compared with products that are not considered to be creations. I submit that we find things to be identifiable and partially describable in terms of clustered characteristics. Further, when we identify, we attend to something that does not vanish (perceptually or conceptually) before we have completed the act of identification. This calls attention to the observation that there is a structure that appears and is identified. But once this is seen, we are led to the further observation that an identity not bound by time, a Form, is present, "grounding" the structure.[11] To challenge this is to introduce theoretical interpretation of what appears, though to affirm it is admittedly to develop description in a more explicitly interpretive way than a description that is purportedly restricted to uninterpreted observation.

In looking at pencils and paintings, or, more generally, in trying to describe created objects by characterizing them, and using examples to do so, my beginning has affinity to a phenomenological approach. And in a loose sense, the beginning is phenomenological. Although it does not include any systematic bracketing, or any deliberately introduced methodological principles, this beginning does require that we initially look at the

---

[11] Let me here appeal to authority – to Plato, particularly in certain implications of the *Theatetus,* or to Peirce, in his later pragmatism, or pragmaticism, where he explains his commitment to generals and his rejection of nominalism. This appeal, of course, is not proof. However, the Platonism involved in my view is not unique, and a defense of the theoretical considerations behind the descriptive claim that identification consists in apprehending identities that are independent of time would require an extended excursion into metaphysics.

phenomenon to be studied with as few explanatory assumptions as possible. I begin with the hope of describing things adequately without initially imposing on them a preconstructed total theory. My hope, then, is to start with observations that are granted by anyone else who also looks. With such observations as a start, what follows unavoidably introduces increasingly explicit interpretive considerations – and finally, a theoretical framework that seems to me to "flow" from the initial observations. But in the present chapter I try throughout to avoid as much as possible departing from these observations. That is, I insist that the conceptual scheme I propose (whatever it may be) apply as directly as possible to the data with which the scheme began.

2. Form

a. Form, structures, and valuation

The foregoing remarks should make it evident that in characterizing Novelty Proper, I presuppose that we have at least an intuitive understanding in ordinary experience of intelligible identities which are encountered as structures and Forms. The description of Novelty Proper affirms that there are in experience intelligible objects of thought, or structures and Forms, and that structures may be exhibited and Forms exemplified in things. The concepts of Form and structure are crucial for the defense of the thesis that we can recognize radical, as distinct from numerical, novelty. However, there are several issues raised by the introduction of the notion of Form and its relation to Novelty Proper, and these must be examined further.

I have said that a Form is an intelligible identity, an object of cognition constituted as a pattern or matrix that enables us to account for the endurance of one or more structures. The term "Form" as I use it, then, shares meaning with a number of different uses. There is a sense in which the term "Form" has as its model repeatable visual shapes. And it is true that the term may refer to these. However, its meaning should not be restricted to the intelligibility of visual patterns. Other kinds of organizations or complexes (other kinds of structures) exemplify Forms. Thus, certain sequences of sounds occur as complexes or structures that exemplify Forms, as in the case of words and of sentences exemplifying propositions. In the case of music, tones may function together so as to exemplify certain musical Forms. Most generally, the term "Form" refers to that in virtue of which a cluster of items – a group of things or of already identified characteristics – cohere sufficiently to be recognized, identified, and subsequently characterized. Once this coherence is discerned, the cluster appears to be an object with a structure, and identification of the structure depends upon an identity or Form which the structured object exemplifies.

It should be pointed out also that an absolutely definite Form is an ideal. As an ideal, a Form is a definite determination, a perfectly coherent and self-consistent unity. But an ideal unity is not an actual unity. Moreover, the absolute definiteness or ideal unity of the Form need not be known. Rather, we need only acknowledge that it functions as a condition. In this sense, it need only be discerned through a variation on, and sometimes an approximation of, this ideal definiteness. As an approximation, a Form is manifest with a degree indeterminacy or vagueness. The identity of the structures of objects we call "cups," for instance, has indeterminate boundaries, and it is doubtful whether any formula could be offered for the exact dimensions of an ideal cup. However, vagueness cannot be so dominant that the Form as discerned completely lacks character. The cluster of items that exemplify it must disclose a coherence sufficient to yield an identity in difference – an identity which, I think, presupposes ideal unity even if the unity sometimes eludes exact specification. If this were not so, then we would have no basis for the consistent application of the term "cup." Moreover, not every object or group of objects exhibits a pattern that is recognized in terms of an intelligible identity. Not every aggregate is sufficiently coherent to appear as exemplifying a Form. And only on rare occasions is a coherent structure sufficiently different as a structure for it to appear as radically new and thus to be a structure that newly discloses a Form.

It is important to acknowledge that the use of the terms "coherence" and "ideal unity" suggest that the identification of a Form depends upon a kind of valuation. Not only is coherence a criterion of the presence of structure, but it also must serve to call attention to itself. If consciousness functions cognitively, if thought takes place, the object of cognition must be sufficiently attractive to be noticed and cognized. The way the object attracts intelligence is linked with the way intelligence regards its object and – though we may be aware of their role later – the purposes for which the object is attended to. This point does not commit us to the view that the object is purely subjective in origin. Whatever our way of attending and whatever our purposes, the object attended to offers itself as something with a certain resistance and character. Nevertheless, cognition depends upon attention and selective discrimination of something in the field of awareness. When cognition takes place, what might be called an epistemological valuation occurs. When consciousness begins to function cognitively, it does so by descrying sufficient definiteness in some focal point in its field so that an object not only is noticed, but in addition, is the basis for something that is recognized and identifiable. Such definiteness is a requirement, and in that sense a value, that conditions the cognizability of the object and that invites cognitive attention.

Let me elaborate this point briefly. Everything and every combination or aggregate which is an object for consciousness must be discriminable. Thus, in order to appear for consciousness at all, the thing or aggregate must at least appear as definite. It must be definite at least as an appearance of an individual. And all things, in this minimal way, exemplify order, the order of being distinct. Yet if the object appears to have no more than the vague character which it must have in order to be noticed, the object does not have sufficient order to render it intelligible in its character. It would not be sufficiently coherent to set it off as a structure and as an exemplification of a Form distinct from, and in various ways related to, other Forms. It would not exhibit sufficient character either to be classifiable or to be contrasted with classified objects. Consequently, the thing which is not merely noticed but is also attended to and recognized as having specific character must be valuable in the minimal sense that in its character it is selected for sustained attention. An object with some degree of definite character attracts attention because its coherence requires that it be noticed and compared with other definite characters.

It might be asked whether the occurence of a new value rather than a new Form is not, after all, what is intended by the notion of Novelty Proper. Why complicate the account of newness by drawing on the notion of Form and the many issues it raises? In response, I must point out that if "Novelty Proper" is construed simply as "first occurrence of value," the recognition that a specific value occurs for the first time would nevertheless depend upon discriminating and distinguishing the value from those in its past. Recognition of the value as different, then, requires discriminating its identity, apprehending a Form that gives the values specificity and character. Newness must initially be recognized in the newness of the exemplification of a Form, even though the Form is valued and the associated value seems new. In short, unless what were claimed to be a new value were intelligible, it could be recognized neither as new nor as a specific value.

b. Form and novelty, some problems and puzzles [12]

The concept of Novelty Proper raises a number of difficult philosophical problems. Some of these problems surely have already become evident, and some of them already have been broached. Although full treatment of these is matter for a systematic study in metaphysics, brief attention to them here should help to sharpen the concept of Novelty Proper. The first philosophical problem that should be acknowledged concerns whether the description of radical newness is bound to the questionable view that Forms are real entities in nature. If so, must I not defend a version of Platonism against the charge that what I refer to as Forms are conceptual entities or perhaps only linguistic tokens?

For the purposes of our discussion, I must reiterate the point that my approach is to begin with what is given. Therefore, it is not at this stage necessary to make a commitment to a view of the status of Forms in reality. My reply to the question, then, is that whatever the status of Forms, recognition of the identities which I call "Forms" does occur. Whether what is recognized must be described or explained in terms of realism, conceptualism, nominalism, or some combination of these theories is not a question that needs to be answered in a description of what appears to be exhibited in instances of radical novelty. Agreement that structures that are dependent upon identities or modes of order at least appear for apprehension is all that is required for the argument. And even if Forms are interpreted as nothing but linguistic phenomena, those that appear for the first time would be characterizable as instances of Novelty Proper.[13]

There is, however, a related problem suggested by this issue. It might be argued that the concept of Novelty Proper is paradoxical if not nonsensical, because it depends upon the problematic relation of Forms which are atemporal to structures and concrete objects which are temporal. In order to provide intelligibility to things that exemplify them, Forms must be abstractable and characterizable in distinction from their instances. They must be constant relative to the concrete moment of initial recognition. They must be atemporal and in this sense transcend their instances. Alternatively, it seems, the fact that an object appears at a moment of time does not contribute to the intelligibility of the object or its structure, and recognition that a Form is exemplified for the first time (that what it

---

[12] The reader who is not concerned with the more general philosophical perplexities that are implied by my account may wish to turn to p. 39, where the main discussion is resumed.

[13] Once again, it must be emphasized that this initial metaphysical neutrality will be abandoned in the succeeding chapters.

makes intelligible is new) must be excluded from the recognition and the identity of the Form. In short, Forms by nature exclude novelty. My account of Form, then, seems to be in conflict with the concept of Novelty Proper. Or more precisely, it may seem that the concept of Novelty Proper purports to make what is atemporal understandable in terms of a temporal locus. The fact that a Form is exemplified at a certain moment in time seems to determine one of its properties, namely its newness. On the other hand, if temporal considerations are irrelevant to the intelligibility of what is new, then Novelty Proper depends upon conditions that are not intelligible.

Another way to make this point lies in observing that creativity is relegated to what is temporal and unintelligible, because it issues in structures that are new. Structures endure in time, and are not, without Forms, intelligible. But since Forms are atemporal, they cannot be new. Hence, newness cannot be intelligible.

The defense of the concept of Novelty Proper in the face of this problem is necessary, for it raises basic issues about what explanation and intelligibility are and how these can be made relevant to creativity. This issue lies at the heart of the reflections offered in later chapters. In the context of this chapter, however, it is necessary to consider the relation of the difficulty to the acceptability of the concept of Novelty Proper.

I do not think that identifying radical newness through the concept of Novelty Proper needs to be abandoned. In the first place, the difficulty of accounting for the way Forms (which are atemporal) can be relevant to novelty (which involves time), though admittedly a fundamental puzzle, simply points to the distinction between the concept of Form and the concept of newness. Apprehending an instance of Novelty Proper requires, first, that a structure be discriminated and a Form be descried, and secondly, that the structure and Form be identified as different from other structures and Forms. For example, a painting in Cézanne's mature style is seen to be an instance of radical newness through seeing its style and its difference from all other known styles of paintings. But identifying such a difference is not the same as recognition of the intelligibility of the different Form. Thus, the intelligibility of the painting is evident in its specific style. The intelligibility of the structure and the Form does not depend upon its being an instance of Novelty Proper. Rather, it depends upon the coherence present in the Form considered in its own right. But this does not negate the requirement that apprehending radical newness depends upon viewing the structure and the Form in a context. It is true that the context has a temporal element. A Form exemplified for the first time is intelligible in a temporal context; yet the difference between the new structure (that newly exemplifies the Form) and other past structures is in part a temporal difference. The comparison that discloses novelty concerns a structure and a Form confronted in the present in relation to structures and Forms confronted in both the present and the past.[14] Occurrences of Novelty Proper are both timeless and temporal. Novelty Proper bridges timeless being and temporal actuality. In this way, Novelty Proper is archetypal of all identities in difference, where some of the differences are discerned in terms of the past and present. At bottom, what is at issue here concerns the status of Novelty Proper rather than the possibility of its including what is temporal as well as what is atemporal. Is Novelty Proper itself a Form? If so, how does the temporal comparison that is part of it relate to what it is as a Form? The problem, of course, is like that of interpreting the concept of time itself on the basis of a view that all concepts have their significance in Forms.

Let me emphasize that I do not claim to have resolved the problem of relating atemporality to temporality. The twofold status of radical novelty may be puzzling, even paradoxical. Nevertheless, this twofold status and the puzzle are implied by what appears in experience on those occasions when a new kind of thing is recognized as what appears for the first time.

Of course, it may still be asked how a Form that is different or that is not characterizable in terms of familiar data can be intelligible or even recognized. And this question also raises another basic problem. But I do not think it should be avoided by denying either that radical novelty occurs or that it can be apprehended by human consciousness. Such a denial would either wholly exclude novelty from the world or it would locate novelty exclusively in unprecedented, unrepeatable individuals construed as unidentifiable because unrelatable to anything else. But surely our finite minds do encounter coherent patterns that are, in the moment of encounter, identities somehow intelligible even though singular and previously unfamiliar.

There is an issue that may be raised from a different perspective than that which affirms that intelligibility requires atemporal identity or Form. This other perspective insists on the intelligibility of what is in continuous flux. It will be given a place in my later discussion of understanding creativity through distinct models of intelligibility. However, in the present context, I must speak to the alternative proposal, because it implies that

[14] There is a sense in which the future is also taken into account, for an instance of Novelty Proper, if also a creation, introduces into the world something that may serve as a prototype, a model that influences the future. But this point must be considered later.

Forms have no place in understanding radical novelty. From this alternative perspective, it might be objected that in insisting that radical novelty requires Form, I have overlooked the continuity that pervades all processes, including creative process. By insisting on the role of Form in characterizing radical novelty, I have artificially conceptualized and separated products from their backgrounds. I have thus overlooked the principle that all processes flow – that change occurs through a definite temporal sequence according to a persistent, uninterrupted continuum and that the result of a process is continuous with the process. The principle of continuity, of course, means that what is intelligible can include no leaps. There is change, but change is not discontinuous.

In response to this objection, it should be emphasized from the beginning that the concept of Novelty Proper does not imply that processes generally do not occur as continuous developments. Most processes may very well be continuous from beginning to end and, in turn, they may be considered continuous with other processes. Moreover, the concept of Novelty Proper does not wholly exclude continuities from those processes that terminate in newly exemplified Forms. Certainly an evolutionary process in which newly exemplified Forms are introduced is developmental and inclusive of many continuities, no matter how sharply its stages may be distinguished. What the concept of Novelty Proper does imply, however, is that at some point in the continuous development of a special kind of process – namely, creative process – there is a break in continuity, a break in the structure of the process. Thus, unlike the steady development of an acorn into an oak tree according to a pattern of change, a process that issues in Novelty Proper is not in every respect continuous. It is not continuous with respect to its structure, that is, with respect to its instancing of the patterns that disclose its intelligibility at the beginning and that disclose its intelligibility at the end (or at the provisional terminus) of the process. The initial ordering of experience of Cézanne before he began to paint is different from the ordering of his experience when he completed his painting, no matter how continuous was the actual process in which he engaged while painting. If we do not admit structural transformations of this kind, we must, I think, treat every product as an antetype, which is to deny radical novelty by assuming that all products and all things are prefigured. Thus, we must be deluded about what appears at the end of a continuous process as a structure that is different in intelligibility from what was intelligible in the past.

Let us look more closely at the claim that a process which issues in novelty consists in unbroken, uninterrupted continuity. What exactly is the continuity of the process? Is it the process considered as whole? Is it the process itself? But surely a process is not identical with its continuity. To be sure, a mathematical series may be construed as a continuum, if all parts of the series are related by infinitesimal intervals. But a process is a series of events which have a qualitative character, while the continuity is properly attributable to, rather than identified with, the process as a whole. Even if the process is construed as indivisible, it has features all of which are not reducible to a collection of items in a series such as infinitesimal intervals in a continuous line. The features of the process give the process a character, and it is the process with a certain character to which "continuity" is attributed. It should be observed, however, that even if it were appropriate to identify a continuum with a process as a whole, I see no way of identifying Novelty Proper either within, or at the terminus of, the continuum without acknowledging a difference between a new aspect of the process and all aspects of the process prior to the advent of what is new in the process. There must be a difference between the continuum after it has reached a new stage and the continuum extending into a past in which the new aspect was not present as part of the intelligible world. If one claimed to find newness in a continuum without this acknowledgement, one would necessarily suppose newness to be present throughout the continuum, and, if all processes are continuous, newness would then be continued as present from all time, past, present, and future. Consequently, no distinction between the old and the new could be made.

Let us suppose that continuities are not identical with the processes said to be continuous. Suppose, then, that continuities are features of processes – features sustained throughout the processes, from their beginnings to their completion. Now, if a continuous process is one in which change occurs, what is the relation of the change to the continuity said to characterize or qualify the process? The continuity as a character must either change or remain constant throughout the process.

On the first alternative, the continuity could not be the same at the end as it was at the beginning of the process; it must undergo interruption, and it must include differences at some point in the process. Thus, the continuity includes breaks with respect to its own character, and my concept of Novelty Proper can be preserved.

On the second alternative, according to which continuities are unchanging characters, the unchanging continuity must either be one of the properties of the process or it must be a constant principle of determination – one of the conditions, or the necessary and sufficient condition, of the changes discerned in the process. If the continuity is one of the properties that remains constant, there is room for change discernible in the complex of other properties. Novelty Proper is thus possible. I can claim that a creative artist, for instance, brings about a new structure, or something intelligible that was not present in the world before he created. But acknowledgement of such newness is not to deny that there is a continuity and constancy of many features of his personality as we know it before and after he creates. The newness generated in the act of creation does not conflict with continuities in the process in which creation occurs.

On the other hand, if continuity is not a property, but rather a constant, consistently operative factor that determines what happens throughout change, then it might be said that the characteristics of the process at the terminus and at the beginning would be different yet related by the constant factor of continuity. The intelligible character of the process at the beginning and the character of the process at the end are both conditioned by the principle of determination which conditions the manner in which the change occurs. On this interpretation, we can acknowledge that there is indeed a difference to be noted in the process; nevertheless, the principle of continuity, which is a determining principle, requires a general developmental structure given at the outset of the process that binds beginning and end in an unbroken continuity. The manner of development, determined by the principle of change, abides and continuity is sustained. Thus, genetic coding may be said to condition the growth of an organism. Environmental factors contribute to a degree of variability, but the genetic coding determines general structural features and general patterns of development.

But does this kind of continuity hold in processes in which something newly intelligible is introduced? I think not. For if we admit that the novelty appears in the result of a process, then the principle that conditions the general developmental structure of the process could not abide as the same throughout all of its stages. Not only is the character of the process different at the end, but where newness appears, this character is not given according to the initial requirements of the developmental structure. If a new structure appears at the end of the process, then the principle determining the general developmental structure must either change prior to the completion of the process or it must include within itself a condition that change occur. But if it includes the requirement that change occur such that the change yields a new structure, and since a new structure is newly intelligible, then the principle cannot, insofar as it is intelligible at the inception of the process, be fully determinant of the structure that is newly intelligible. If the genetic coding of an organism includes a condition for a new structure, then the genetic coding must include a condition for its own modification. It could not then remain constant throughout a creative process.

Thus, I insist that the intelligible character of a process that includes radical novelty is different at some distinct stage of these processes; and some of the continuities in the processes, so far as they are intelligible, are disconnected at some point between the beginning and terminus of the process. Not only does the character of the process change, but it changes according to a changing principle of growth. If this point is denied, then the appearance of intelligible, identifiable difference, and radical novelty, must be either denied or interpreted as illusory.

Let me make the point from a different perspective. The term "continuity" characterizes the course of a process as unbroken, yet also unfixed. To identify an aspect of process in this way is to give it character and to consider it in terms of an intelligible principle. But once process is so viewed, it is viewed steadily. The fluidity we try to insist upon in the process is frozen under the steady reference of our characterization. To be sure, it remains frozen, we say, only so long as we conceptualize by means of the term "continuity." After all, the term itself is intended to call attention to the unfrozen, to the flow of process. But if this is the only function of the term "continuity," then it simply calls attention to the observation that processes are alterations. Most important, however, is that once a closer view is taken of what is said to be changing, yet continuous, that which is intelligible in it is marked off, is made to stand still to be recognized as different from what, at least phenomenally, was required by whatever structure gave specific intelligibility to the process prior to the change. The concept of continuity is, I think, a covert way of acknowledging Form, at least in instances of radical newness.

B. NOVELTY PROPER AND CREATIVE ACTS

On the assumption that the concept of Novelty Proper is acceptable in its essentials, let us explore its applicabillity in a characterization of creative acts. An initial application of this concept suggests that everything that is an instance of Novelty Proper – everything that newly exemplifies a Form disclosed through a new structure – is a created object, and the act or process which issues in Novelty Proper is creative. An act which is creative must generate new structure and lead to the discovery of an unknown Form. This suggestion is a straightforward application, and I think it reflects a conventional way of regarding creative acts.

However, the mere presence of Novelty Proper in a product does not warrant our calling the product a "created object." Nor does the production of Novelty Proper guarantee that the process is "creative." This first description, then, needs to be qualified.

1. Imitation and Craftsmanship

The proposal that a creative act must lead to Novelty Proper seems to exclude the works of craftsmen and artists who, though they are called "creative," conform to a style already known to them. It might be said, for example, that the requirement rules out the possibility that much ancient Egyptian art is "creative"; for most artists of that period conformed to a familiar formula or pattern – a Form already known and thus not new. This argument, of course, depends upon the assumption that craftsmen and artists who restrict themselves to one style do not produce Novelty Proper, because they follow conventions and their work is stylized and repetitious. I would suggest, however, that the term "creative" is appropriately applied to these artists and craftsmen precisely to the extent that they, or those leaders whom they followed, have surpassed routine duplication of established conventions. Thus, the products of creative craftmanship invite us to recognize a new Form in the subtleties of the finished work.[15] Accordingly, our admiration of the "creative" ability of Egyptian artists lies in our recognition of variations and nuances that are relevant to different Forms within established or conventionally acknowledged Forms. Evidence of the role of refined variations within traditions that are thought to be highly stylized and conventional is obvious in contemporary oriental art. Japanese potters, for instance, repeat over and over certain basic shapes. Yet they strive for a perfection of these shapes through variations in execution. Moreover, some of these variations, when deemed successful, are admired as innovations on the patterns which they strive to perfect.

Of course, there are some of us with less discriminating eyes who may fail to see these variations. And there may well be examples that reveal very little deviation from convention, yet which still are considered important evidence of Egyptian creativity. If one were to deny that such examples show any significant variation on conventions, why should we take these to be "creative?" Do we attribute the term "creative" to them

[15] On being "invited" to see novelty, see Robert B. Macleod, "Retrospect and Prospect," Chapter 6, *Contemporary Approaches to Creative Thinking*, edited by Howard E. Gruber, Glenn Terrell, Michael Wertheimer (New York: Atherton Press, 1962), p. 182.

simply because they are crafts, because they are the products of trained human effort? If this were the reason, then "creative" would mean nothing more than "well made," even if what is made were the product of an assembly line. Yet I do not think we regard Egyptian art as created simply because it is well made. I think there is reason to regard Egyptian art as creative in the sense of radical creation even when we overlook subtle variation, and this is possible because of the concept of Novelty Proper. We sometimes conceive, not of individual Egyptian artists, but rather of an entire age as creative, or as it might be put, of "the" Egyptian artist as creative, because the age itself, rather than individual artists, newly exemplified a Form in the tradition. Thus Novelty Proper is attributable to the general Form of a period with respect to its difference from Forms of earlier periods.

Further, the point that craftsmen may be considered original in the sense of producing radically new results is shown in our recognition that some of those artists we consider extraordinary in creativity, such as Michelangelo, looked on themselves as craftsmen. In short, I am insisting that artists who adhere to formerly realized styles are deemed creative either because their work is associated with a process that already produced the style for the first time, or because each of their works, done in accordance with a prefigured style, has its own individual coherent unity and its own Novelty Proper.

In any case, even if the initial proposal that creative acts must produce Novelty Proper did exclude craftsmen, Egyptian artists, and artists who repeat themselves (and I think it does not exclude them), the primary issue here concerns those instances in which creation advances beyond what was previously known. And the use of the concept of Novelty Proper is an attempt to do justice to the latter kind of creativity. The objection, after all, is significant only if it is intended to show that all artists are creative by virtue of imitating the past, or that no creator transcends his heritage. But surely there is a difference between "creative artists" who only conform to conventions and "creative artists" who initiate new conventions.

2. *Creative Process and Critical Control*

If the requirement that a creative process must yield Novelty Proper does not exclude craftsmanship, it does seem to be too broad; for it does not exclude certain kinds of accidental processes. For example, according to our description thus far, an array of pieces of glass fallen from a window broken by an inaccurately thrown baseball might seem to be "created" if it appeared to present an intelligible visual principle or order. But though the boy who threw the ball would be responsible for the array, he could hardly be called responsible for the coherent form or Novelty Proper in the sense that he would be deemed "creative" of it. In this case, it might be said that no human created the result; it would be an accident discovered by the observer.

But surely, someone will say, a person who happens to see the shattered glass and who discerns a coherent pattern, deserves to be thought of as creative. Such a person would be a creative observer; and this is what all of us must be in our aesthetic responses to natural objects and to critically constructed as well as accidentally produced man-made objects. The answer to this proposal has already been implied. It was said that whether Forms have a status within, dependent upon, or independent of, our minds need not be decided before we attempt to characterize Novelty Proper. Whatever the status of the Forms that condition the identification of things, we can nevertheless consider the relations of these Forms to what they make intelligible. Similarly, we can also specify the criteria by virtue of which an activity, no matter whose activity it is, is creative. Thus it would not be inconsistent with the characterization of creativity given thus far to admit that an observer who discerns Novelty Proper in the array of glass is creative. Even the boy who inadvertently broke the window might be considered creative, if he had the courage to survey the result of his deed and in doing so recognized Novelty Proper. And, in that case, the creative process, I take it, would not be the act of throwing the baseball, but rather the discriminating act of observation – an act in which a critical, controlled "seeing" operates in the recognition of Form.

Yet surely a distinction needs to be made. We do distinguish between Forms for which observers are responsible and Forms for which another agent is responsible and which are made available for the observer's eyes. It is the latter kind of Form which is ordinarily associated with creative artists or, more generally, creative agents. Thus, if an observer can indeed be creative, he is not ordinarily thought of as a creative agent unless he at least communicates to an audience his recognition of Novelty Proper. Further, this kind of communication must be effected through some controlled use of a medium such as words, visual qualities, bodily motions, musical tones, etc. Accordingly, I take it for granted that the creative activity which at bottom is in question is that of an agent who is responsible for Novelty Proper by virtue of some conscious effort.

The first qualification needed for the characterization, then, is that the process must manifest some control and direction on the part of the agent. A process that is creative must include critical, attentive effort that is relevent to the new structure that issues from the process. The agent must be responsible for the outcome, and the outcome must issue in Novelty Proper.[16]

This characterization of creative acts, however, may be accepted only with additional qualification. It is apparent that the assumption with which this chapter began insists that the radical novelty in question marks a break in continuities – a gap between what was already established and what is new. From the standpoint of our understanding, the order and direction must be discontinuous and not wholly preconceived. Indeed, in some instances of human creativity, whatever direction is present may be unrecognized by consciousness until the creation appears to be complete. The sudden occurrence of a whole musical composition, or a substantial part of it, to the consciousness of Mozart can hardly be called consciously directed or ordered before it appeared. And long periods of forgetting a task, followed by sudden illumination, suggest that the creator did not consciously control and direct all of the phases of the creative process.[17] Further, cases in which serendipity is apparent, as in Pasteur's discovery of vaccine, seems to belie the qualification that every creative process must be fully directed and controlled.

Does this insistence on discontinuity and disruption of order and control reintroduce the admission that creations are simply accidents? I think not. For the discontinuities occur in contexts in which order and control operate. Thus, the traceable qualities of the created product can be seen as coherent with the past, while that which is not fully traceable, that is, the Form and structure of the instance of Novelty Proper, is not incoherent with the possibility of an ordered development in the future. The direction given the process by the creator may be the critical control exercised once the creator has recognized the new Form and decides to accept rather than reject it.[18] Or, if processes in nature are in question, direction may be given in the relation of a new Form – a species, in this case – to a process of evolution that leads to and gains meaning from the Form. A change that remains only a "mutation," by contrast, would be a new individual that

---

[16] R. G. Collingwood, *op. cit.*, pp. 125-135, Vincent Tomas, "Creativity in Art," *The Philosophical Review*, LXVII, No. 1 (January, 1958), pp. 1-15.

[17] Graham Wallas' widely accepted description of incubation as one of the stages of the creative process emphasizes the point that the creator is not in full control of at least some phases of the creative act. See *The Art of Thought* (New York: Harcourt, Brace, and Company, 1926).

[18] That acceptance or rejection of the final result is a form of critical control is argued by Tomas, *op. cit.*

is not sustained and appropriated into biological evolution. In short, if occurrences of Novelty Proper are accidents, they are not accidents in the sense of sheer deviations. They must be at the very least intelligible accidents — accidents not intelligible because understandable with reference to antecedents but because they are controlled, because they manifest their own new intelligibility, and because they contribute to an ordered future.

3. Creative Achievement and Duplication of Novelty

But what are we to say about two or more processes that issue independently in similar or identically new Forms — in products that cannot strictly both be examples of Novelty Proper, yet which issue from processes that are and seem rightly to be called "creative"? The evolution of the same species of life in two different parts of the universe presumably would both be creative (if any processes in nature are creative). Or, in human creativity, it is well known that Darwin's theory of evolution published in 1859 did not exemplify a structural pattern which, without qualification, manifested Novelty Proper. A. R. Wallace, working independently, originated a theory which is basically the same as Darwin's. Similarly, Leibniz and Newton are said to have developed the infinitesimal calculus, each without full knowledge of the work of the other. In these examples, the processes seem to be properly called "creative"; yet, because one of them in each pair occurred second in time, presumably it could not strictly manifest Novelty Proper. If two theories have the same structure, and one is constructed prior to the other, it seems that both cannot manifest radical newness.[19]

This objection cannot be answered adequately by saying simply that each agent can be called creative relative to his own knowledge and consciousness of Novelty Proper. For the consequence of regarding a process as creative if the result only appears to the agent to yield Novelty Proper is that every discovery, that of a retarded child as well as that of

---

[19] One might respond here by claiming that no two theories are exactly alike, and no two creations exemplify the same Form; thus, the theories in their subtleties are different and both men are creative. Or it might be argued that Leibniz and Newton did have some knowledge of each others' work, as did Wallace and Darwin. Consequently, they must be regarded either as mutual plagiarists or as collaborators. Finally, it might be argued that just the extent to which they did not have acquaintance with each others' thoughts, is the extent to which there are variations and thus there is no duplication in their creations. These responses may preserve my characterization of creativity by means of the concept of Novelty Proper. However, duplication of creation in independent processes is a possibility, and some believe it has occurred. My description can be defended while such duplication is admtted.

an eminent investigator, would be creative. All learning would count as creative, for the Form learned would be a new Form for the learner. Many who inquire about creativity would of course welcome this consequence. But if a retarded child's learning process is creative, it is not creative as is the work of those who provide the model for creativity – in the way Darwin, Newton, Giotto, or Beethoven are creative. The learning process can be creative, at best, only in a derivative sense.

There are two qualifications that distinguish creative activity from ordinary learning. The first will be introduced here, and the second will be discussed in the concluding section. A process which is creative must be productive of a new Form that is relative not only to the consciousness of the agent of the process, but also to the orderly development of processes leading to, and rationally relevant to, the agent's activity. What may be called "a vertical dimension" of the tradition of work prior to the creative advance yields a break after which Novelty Proper appears. Thus, given the "horizontal dimension" that provides background data available to the agent before creation, and given assumptions about the normal capabilities of agents, there is introduced a vertical thrust, a leap, seen in the novelty for which he is responsible. This novelty is unpredictable and not traceable to past data and the agent's ordinary capabilities. By contrast, given capabilities and data known to be available to the "non-creative" agent, the "novelty" for which he is responsible is precedented and seems predictable, at least in principle, and traceable to the process leading to the agent's achievement. We can predict what persons at various ages, given certain information, will learn. And we can trace what appears as novel for them to prior data and capabilities in their development.[20]

Thus, if two processes lead independently to the "same" results as in the case of Wallace and Darwin, the processes are perhaps less striking, but the creative character of neither is dimished as long as each in its vertical development yields Novelty Proper for its tradition – that is, as long as

---

[20] I must emphasize again that to insist on the irreducibility of Novelty Proper to antecedents within a tradition is not to say that there are no rational connections whatsoever to be found between the new structure and its past. As Norwood Hanson has recently argued convincingly, there are patterns of discovery in science. See *Patterns of Discovery, An Inquiry into the Conceptual Foundations of Science* (Cambridge: Cambridge University Press, 1961). And similar claims have been made for art. However, those rational connections or patterns that can be identified appear after the discovery has been made, when we can look back on the relation of the result to past knowledge. They do not disclose themselves to the creator or to us until the new idea is made communicable through a set of concepts or through the new Forms which have advanced the tradition. Furthermore, there remains the irreducible novelty of the altered or new assumptions which are required for the formation of the new idea. And these assumptions break with the rational course of an established tradition.

each is not only relative subjectively, to what each of the agents knew, but also relative objectively, to a development of activity that could not have been expected to lead to the outcome.

C. VALUE AND CREATIVITY

The final qualification of our characterization of creativity is that a process which is creative must issue in something valuable.[21] Mere difference of structure does not guarantee that the structure is a creation. Merely being eccentric is not necessarily being creative. The presence of value as a condition of creativity was explicitly suggested earlier in the discussion of Novelty Proper. It was claimed that cognizance of Form depends upon valuation in the sense of selection. Thus, a Form or identity in difference presents a kind of value insofar as the coherence that reveals it makes possible the appearance and selection of what is discriminable and intelligible. The relevance of value to intelligibility must now be explored. It was also suggested that value is present in created objects because control and responsibility enter creative acts and because creativity must yield products that are either contributions to, or at least not incoherent with, traditions in their futures. I shall conclude this chapter by sketching a proposal for specifying the role value plays in identifying created objects and in the development of creative processes. This proposal presupposes a general theory of value which I shall only adumbrate.

In a consideration of the relation of value to creativity, two features of creative acts should be emphasized. On the one hand, the agent does not begin a creative process with a preconception of the explicit structure of the end toward which his act is directed. On the other hand, the agent in some way is responsible for the new Form that appears in relation to the creative process. Thus, an artist struggles to effect something the exact character of which he does not envisage. Yet he does know when he has achieved that for which he struggled. He does know when all requirements have been met. His critical judgment determines the moment at which the process is complete and whether what has been completed is acceptable to him. These two features will be seen to be crucial to the following suggestions concerning value and creativity.

Creativity includes an element of discovery and an element of control.

---

[21] In this discussion, I shall adopt the terminology that employs "value" and "disvalue" rather than "good and "bad," or "beautiful" and "ugly." This terminology, which has developed in the context of modern moral and aesthetic theories, presupposes that a distinction can be made between what is and what ought to be. This distinction should be clearer in the discussion to follow.

Thus, it is neither the production of what was familiar nor simply the discovery of what was unfamiliar. Creative processes lead to discoveries and the production of unfamiliar results which are also valuable. Consequently, Novelty Proper is not deemed a mark of creativity unless the product that exhibits it is also valuable. What kind of value is attributable to created objects? The answer requires that we draw on the familiar distinction between instrumental and intrinsic or inherent values.[22] Both kinds of value are fundamental for creativity; but one of them, inherent value, is more fundamental and indispensable in the identification and the development of creative processes. However, let us first consider briefly how we might conceive of created objects as exemplifying instrumental value.

1. Instrumental Value

Although it is not possible here to enumerate the many senses of the concept of instrumental value, two of them should be noted: extrinsic and utilitarian. Extrinsic value is valuable in the sense of being a necessary condition for the realization of another value which is not an immediate need but which lies in the future. Utility is valuable in the sense of meeting an immediate need or purpose. Thus, a thing may be instrumentally valuable in its usefulness for some purpose at hand; as such, it is of utilitarian value. Further, its utility may be different from the kind of purpose for which the useful thing is ordinarily the instrument. Such transformation of utility may or may not yield Novelty Proper. An automobile, for example, was once, for the first time, made valuable simply as a shelter during a rain storm. This utilitarian value of the car is not necessary to its primary function. The purpose of obtaining shelter would be fulfilled even if the car did not provide us with a mode of transportation. And a car could run without serving as shelter. The shelter value of the automobile, then, is different with respect to the primary use of automobile. Yet, this functioning as shelter is not an instance of Novelty Proper; for the purpose of obtaining shelter is familiar and the shelter properties of automobiles must already have been evident. Moreover, the combination of the automobile and its shelter value does not yield a new value. The intelligibility of the concept of an automobile as a shelter is not an integration of the

---

[22] Let it be noticed here that I use the term "inherent" in acknowledgement of C. I. Lewis' view that intrinsic values are subjective, while inherent values have the objectivity of the objects to which they are attributable. See C. I. Lewis, *An Analysis of Knowledge and Valuation,* The Paul Carus Lectures, Seventh Series, 1945 (LaSalle, Illinois: The open Court Publishing Company, 1946), pp. 551-554.

value with something new. The resultant does not appear to be more than juxtaposition of its antecedent characteristics, and there is nothing radically new about this shift from a primary to a secondary purpose.

Yet an object also may be found useful in a way that is primary to it and that is different or unfamiliar with respect both to previously known purposes and to the object's formerly primary function. Thus its purpose would be an instance of Novelty Proper, because it would be a function of a structure different from what went before it. And because of its novelty and its value, the object would be deemed created. Pasteur's creation or discovery of vaccine seems thus to be a creation. The use of a spoiled cholera culture to prevent the death of the chickens with which Pasteur was working was a use not originally primary to the culture. The relation of the new to the old purpose of the cholera culture, however, is not like the relation of the subsidiary purpose of the car used for shelter to the primary purpose of the car for transportation. The use of the culture as a vaccine is an instance of both Novelty Proper and ultitarian value and is an example of creativity. Pasteur's creative achievement consisted in recognizing as a primary purpose what might have remained an indirect function – a function of no value because it did not serve his initial experimental ends. Pasteur was creative in substituting a different but valuable use, vaccination, for a familiar use, causing cholera. Novelty Proper, then, may appear in an object whose familiar and primary utilitarian value is replaced by a different utilitarian value which becomes primary to the object and which could not be routinely interpreted.

It should be observed that in the example of Pasteur, because of the kind of instrumental value realized, the new purpose has served as a contribution to human knowledge. Specifically, in its function as vaccine, the cholera culture was also valuable to the development of medicine. Thus, it was more than immediately useful or utilitarian in value. In being instrumental to knowledge, Pasteur's achievement served intrinsic or inherent value. In serving medicine, the discovery was extrinsically valuable.

2. *Instrumental Value and Tradition*

This last point leads to the sugestion that if an instance of Novelty Proper has instrumental value, the new thing must be a contribution to a tradition – a tradition thought to be valuable in its own terms. Thus, a thing may be of instrumental value by newly serving its own kind. A member of a species may serve its offspring and, in turn, its species, without regard to its taking on immediate utilitarian value with respect to other things. It may make such a contribution through exemplifying a new Form that makes intelligible a variation that enhances the species. The realization of this kind of value is sufficient to qualify a result as created, even if utility or immediate instrumental value is absent. This kind of instrumental value of the created object is reflected in terms such as "fruitful," "effective," "important," that are often applied to new results which are thought to be "created" and that are applied without specific reference to utility. The value by virtue of which the created object contributes to a tradition is instrumental in the sense that the creation is a means to a modification of its tradition. The value may lie in the creation's culminating or enhancing a tradition, as did the music of Bach; it may lie in the advancement of a tradition, as did the work of Giotto and Cézanne; or it may lie in prophesying and adding to a tradition far in its future, as did El Greco's painting.

Instrumental value is not something at which a creator necessarily aims deliberately. That the creator does not foresee a contribution before he has finished his work is surely true of the artist, if not always of the inventor or scientist. In art, at least, the tradition is open. The works that advance it determine its nature. Only after the fact can we look back on previous developments as somehow "leading to" or as relevant to the new creation.

Instrumental value, however, is not invariably the kind of value that marks a new object as created in character. A work of art, for instance, may be deemed created although lacking in a clearly defined contribution to a tradition. Some of Picasso's experimental achievements do not seem to have directly influenced the tradition – certainly they participate to a lesser degree than do other styles of his which have been integral to the evolution of painting. Yet these departures do appear to be creations. They are neither sheer eccentricities nor major contributions to the tradition. Why, then, are they deemed created? The answer, I sugest, is that they issue from controlled processes and exemplify both Novelty Proper and a kind of value other than that which is either utilitarian or extrinsically related to a tradition: they exemplify inherent value.

3. *Inherent Value*

Inherent as well as instrumental value may be attributed to created objects. Indeed, the possibility of serving a tradition depends upon the self-sufficiency of the value which can, when appropriated, serve to enhance and advance the tradition which it helps constitute. Only on the basis of self-sufficient value could the new Form of the created object serve as a model that may influence future processes. As a model, the new thing must exhibit a value that is intrinsic or inherent. The kind of value under consideration is that which is encountered in an object rather than in some end the object serves. The created object, then, must be valuable for its own sake. And its inherent value is the condition by virtue of which the created object may become instrumentally valuable in perfecting or advancing, or, in the most radical instances, creating a tradition.

Inherent values may be distinguished into kinds according to their status and their specificity and complexity. Hence, the created object is intrinsically or inherently valuable in at least two ways: (1) as a new being, and (2) as a new kind of being. First, it is valuable simply by virtue of its being, where the term 'being" is used to refer to any determination or discriminable and identifiable object of consciousness. Accordingly, the created object is valuable because it is a determination or coherent structure which exemplifies intelligibility that was not previously known. And this is to exemplify the inherent value of determinateness as such, the value of being an intelligible object without consideration of the respect in which the new object is intelligible. The requirement suggests why we sometimes place value on "novelty," "freshness," "originality" in art, without at the moment deeming it necessary to refer to the precise character of what is original.

This requirement, I think, is also the basis for the creator's directing the creative process toward something the character of which is not yet determined but which is recognized by him as some future determination that ought to be realized.[23] The future determination that ought to be given determination does not provide rules; it does not display criteria for accepting or rejecting ideas or elements. But it does appear as a "requiredness," a demand, and a foundation for the inevitability of the specific Form to be made definite. Thus, the dim presence of a Form as such, before the specificity of the Form is recognized, is an aim that lures the creator. The creator is lured by it because, as a vague and as yet undetermined Form, it marks the beginning of the being of something, something that can have a definite intelligibility and specific value. Since the undetermined Form is the basis for intelligibility, it may be considered as instrumentally valuable to the inherent value of the finished and intelligible Form which will mark the result as a created object. But without the inherent value of simply being something, the requiredness that there be some specific Form would be groundless.

[23] The as yet indefinite ought-to-be functions somewhat as Susanne Langer's "commanding form" in the development of the art process. See *Feeling and Form* (New York: Charles Scribner's Sons, 1953), especially pp. 120 ff.

Someone might, of course, object that not all new things are valuable merely because they are beings. Surely some of the destructive Nazi "innovations" were not valuable because they came into being. But this objection I think, springs from the view that a thing, whether new or old, may be evil (may be a disvalue) without regard to other things. The view I am suggesting assumes that evil is distinguishable from the being of an evil thing and is identifiable only with respect to a conflict between the thing in question and some other determinate object. Thus, I wish to insist that coming into being is in itself of value and that there is no disvalue without a conflict of beings.

The point that coming into being is of value was implied earlier. I said that selection is the foundation for the apprehension of Form. In the sense that the determination of Form appears as demanding identification and characterization, and thus intelligibility, all Forms are valuable in this fundamental sense of the value of being.

Yet, there is a second way in which a created object is inherently valuable. It consists in the exemplification by the object of what Nicolai Hartmann has called the ought-to-be which is a kind of "ideal being." [24] This kind of value is inseparable from the first. It enhances and fills out the value of simply coming into being. And it is essentially related to the structure of the new Form, that is, the specific intelligibility of the novel being. Thus, this kind of inherent value is attributable to a new Form by virtue of the determinate structure of the new object. It appears on condition that the specific and definite Form in question is recognized as what ought to be, not simply because it is something determinate, but also because it is a certain kind of being which is intelligible in a definite way that ought to be. Unless there were an inherent value in the *kind* of structure that occurs for the first time, created objects would be valuable only in the general way all intelligible things are valuable, that is, valuable simply for being. Thus there would be no new values. There would not even be new instrumental values, for there would be no special value attaching to a new kind of purpose.

Inherent value of kind is, of course, correlated with the creative agent's admittedly paradoxical critical direction of the process toward a *kind* of result the details of which he as yet does not completely envisage. Unlike the inherent value of being, value of kind cannot appear to the creator as an aim, since it is not yet determined in such a way as to be the target of that aim. Nor can it provide a set of preconceived criteria by which the process is controlled. Yet, after the fact, after the created object is com-

[24] *Ethics* (New York: The Macmillan Company, 1958), Volume One.

plete, the value of the exemplified Form can be viewed as the condition which fulfilled the creative agent's critical demands, and as that for which he is responsible.

What has been said about the distinct ways inherent values function in the creative process raises a host of questions. How, for instance, is it possible that a creator can critically select and be responsible for a definite Form which he can envisage at best only vaguely before he knows and accepts it? Is the value of being, i.e., is the lure of Form and intelligibility, in some way intimately related to and determinative of inherent value of kind? These are questions which can only be answered in the context of a comprehensive theory, an ontology and a value theory that does justice to radical creativity. Suggestions for the direction of such a comprehensive theory will appear in later chapters. However, a fully adequate development of an ontology and value theory is possible only in another study. For the moment, I must reiterate that the principal purpose of this chapter has been simply to indicate the conditions necessary to identify an act as creative.

Let me conclude with a summary of the characterization of creativity which I have proposed. I have claimed that an act that is creative must meet three conditions. It must appear to be discontinuously directed or controlled, at least in being found acceptable by critical selection. It must issue in Novelty Proper that exhibits inherent value independently of a tradition and that may be relative to a tradition which it enhances, advances, or initiates. Finally, it must yield a product which is valuable in at least two ways, that is, it must be inherently valuable as a determination of a new being and as a kind of determination which merits sustenance.

CHAPTER II

SPONTANEITY: THE PARADOX AND THE POSSIBILITY OF EXPLANATION

INTRODUCTION

Creative acts appear to be anomalies. They appear to be controlled yet discontinuous processes which lead to valuable Novelty Proper and which interrupt the regularity and orderliness expected of an intelligible world.[1] Creativity exhibits a tension between two poles: on the one hand, the presence of spontaneity – of radical, irreducible difference – and on the other hand, the presence of an identity that invites a search for a continuity between creations and their contexts. Newness exhibits the first pole; intelligibility seems to demand the second.

Now the hope of resolving the tension turns on the question whether it is possible to find connections between creations and their historical contexts. The connections may be construed as compelling necessities or simply as regularities. Yet on either alternative, identification of them would provide knowledge that would enable us to foresee creations forthcoming at future times. Such knowledge presupposes predictability as a basic criterion of intelligibility, and the acceptance or rejection of this criterion marks the principal differences among perspectives on creativity. If creative acts can be explained naturalistically, so that the appearance of discontinuity can be rejected, then creations must in some sense be predictable. Those who affirm the possibility of such explanation are in a broad sense rationalists or determinists.[2]

In the following remarks, this point will be explored. I shall attempt to show the extent to which a rationalistic perspective is assumed by a variety

---

[1] I assume, of course, that every instance of Novelty Proper originates in an act. Consequently, where there is Novelty Proper there is a discontinuously developmental act that leads to it. In short, Novelty Proper implies spontaneity and, if value is present, creativity.

[2] The loose sense in which I use the terms "rationalist" and "determinist" has been discussed in the Introduction to this book. It will be indicated further as the discussion progresses.

of philosophical as well as scientifically oriented positions. Several examples of the rationalistic determinist's approach will be discussed, because it is important to see that in spite of their demands for intelligibility, rationalists find it difficult to avoid acknowledging that creativity is paradoxical. Unless they categorically deny the occurrence of newness in any form, they inevitably formulate their views so that they inadvertently acknowledge that creativity eludes rational categories.

In beginning with an examination of the extent to which spontaneity or creativity is the kind of phenomenon that resists rational explanation, I shall abandon the metaphysical neutrality I have tried to maintain throughout the first chapter. The discussion must now be broadened so that it is no longer confined to a description of what appears to us as present in created objects and thus in creative acts. The discussion will concern explanation rather than description.

The turn away from the loose phenomenological approach of the first chapter is crucial. Not only is this turn taken in order to speak to the major issue that has inspired studies of creativity, but it also must be engaged in order to make as clear as possible the extent to which the proposed characterization of creativity is more than a prescription or quasi-nominal definition which suggests that I have "defined" creativity so that it cannot be fully conceptualized or explained by ordinary discursive, rational means. It might be objected, for instance, that the proposed characterization is the basis for begging the question of whether creativity can be explained, since the description I have given, by definition (or by characterization), affirms discontinuities or gaps among those structures by which the world of the creator is understood. And indeed it does affirm discontinuities. But it does so on the basis of a claim about what we find prior to interpretation. The issue at hand now turns on whether the proposed characterization not only is adequate to what appears to occur in situations in which we believe we have seen creative achievement, but is also adequate in the sense that it withstands claims to the effect that "Novelty Proper" refers only to appearances, or illusions, which will be known to be illusions once adequate explanatory theory is brought to bear upon them.

In considering the possibility of explaining creativity, I shall focus on the explanation of creative acts insofar as they yield Novelty Proper, without regard, for the moment, to the value they must disclose as creations. If what I say is plausible for objects and activities regarded independently of the role of value, then it should be no less plausible if we were to introduce the question whether we can explain the value attributed to creations.

If there is reason to reject the proposal that the necessary condition of creativity, Novelty Proper, can be subjected to the criterion of predictability, then the presence of value would not itself make prediction possible. It would instead add to the difficulties of foreseeing creative achievement.

A. GENERAL REMARKS ABOUT EXPLANATION

What do we expect when we hope to understand a phenomenon? The attempt to understand something begins with some apparent disorder – a lack of coherence, a conflict, an anomaly in what is experienced, and an awareness of this discrepancy on the part of the observer.[3] We observe an odd growth on a tree in the garden. The growth is out of place. Consequently, we try to understand it. We read expressions in a foreign language. The words and form seem incoherent with our own linguisthic habits. We try to understand the expression. We know something about the surface of the moon, but its differences from our own terrestrial environment and absence of information about the sub-surfaces of the moon leaves a discrepancy within our knowledge, and we try to gain understanding in order to overcome this discrepancy.

Once a discrepancy provokes the attempt to understand, several alternatives are open to us. One of these is the attempt to understand in the sense of having an explanation, and this kind of understanding will be central. Such understanding may be scientific, or it may simply be consistent with scientiffic explanation. Thus, what will be at issue is a form of explanation that need not be scientific but which nevertheless need not conflict with the special explanations of science.

Understanding, of course, may aim at results not strictly thought of as explanation. It may consist in such tasks as finding "factual" descriptions or classifications – inductive enumerations of properties of members of classes, measurements, or inductive-statistical summaries. Inquiries into such descriptive matters are supportive of explanations.

However, understanding in the sense of explaining is more basic than these in fulfilling our intellectual demands. An explanation is directed toward resolving the discrepancy that provoked thought by answering the questions, How? or Why? How does something that seems out of place occur? Why does it occur as it does? These questions are aimed at identi-

[3] To say that explanation begins with some noticed discrepancy is not to say that all theoretical thinking is problem solving. There are realms of experience, I think, in which understanding may be pursued for the sake of intellectual curiosity or purely non-utilitarian ends. But such understanding is initiated by recognition that something thought about is somehow less coherent than it might be with itself or with its context.

fying a source or origin of the thing to be explained, whether the source is construed as one or more powers, a set of regularities, or one or more principles. Thus the thing to be explained must be related to something else more fundamental relative to it.

Further, that to which the thing to be explained is related – something construed as a source or basis for the thing to be explained – is itself a term in relation to other terms. At minimum, an explanation furnishes a statement about relations among discriminated experiences. Explanation at its best offers a scheme of relations among things and events which include and bring into connections the things or events in which there was a discrepancy. For instance, I may observe an extraordinary number of ants in and near my home. The discrepancy between expectations and observation leads me to explain what I see. Investigation enables me to identify the insects as carpenter ants which form colonies where wood is readily available. I remember that a large pile of dead wood has been under my porch for some time. I then believe I have made at least the first step toward an explanation. And I have done this by connecting a number of items, including a generalization about the behavior of certain kinds of ants and an observation about a particular circumstance, the location of something connected with that behavior. This initial thought about the discrepancy is the first step toward fitting into a system the observation that initiated the search for an explanation. Explanations in meteorology also serve to illustrate this point, even though meteorology has not gone as far as some sciences in building a system that fully systematizes a vast diversity of phenomena. Explanations in fields that do not obviously depend upon explaining discrepancies also illustrate the indispensability of system in explanation. Curiosity about a routine occurrence such as the change in the color of leaves in the fall is promted by observed change and is aimed at relating the kind of change in question to other changes and various circumstances such as pigments and substances that respond to light and temperature variations.

However, it is important to notice what kind of connections are sought. First of all, these connections must constitute a system.[4] To explain is to fit into a coherent scheme. But there are different kinds of system: morphological, nomological, causal. We are concerned with nomological and causal systems, since these are, *prima facie,* systems that are explanatory. Causal systems are the more broadly conceived, for they include morpho-

---

[4]Here I follow Blanshard, *The Nature of Thought* (New York: Humanities Press, 1964), Vol. II, especially pp. 23-36.

logical and nomological considerations as well as connections of causal dependence.[5]

The term "cause" has many meanings, and we should consider the most basic of these which have been proposed. I shall assume some familiarity with Aristotle's identification of four causes: material, efficient, formal, and final. With qualification appropriate to contemporary thought, the concepts of efficient and final causes are prominent in interpretations of what "cause" means. Thus, if explanation appeals to a system that includes causal relations, these causal relations may depend upon efficient or final or both kinds of causes together. For convenience, let me say that in systems in which efficient causes are dominant, the system will be called *mechanistic*.[6] Those systems in which final causes are dominant will be called *teleological*.[7] Let us now briefly consider efficient and final causes and their roles in the kinds of systems in which they are dominant.

Efficient causes may be construed as (1) productive agents, (2) principles that necessitate effects, or (3) regularly correlated events. These types of interpretations can be traced to philosophical rationalism, empiricism, and variations on both of these which have been proposed by twentieth century philosophies of science. It should be evident that I cannot here do justice to all of the intricacies of these views of cause. But I do wish to highlight certain necessary features of them for the purpose of describing mechanistic explanation and its relevance for understanding creative acts.

The view that an efficient cause is an agent or productive condition is generally thought to have been derived from human experiences of acts of will. To will something includes a feeling of effort that is continuous with bringing about some effect. Thus, any thing or event that is to be explained would, on this view, be traceable to a productive agent. And in such an explanation, the system into which the conflict to be resolved would fit is an ordered pattern of productive acts and their effects.

The view that a cause is that which necessitates is allied to a rational-

---

[5] The use of the term "cause," of course, has been challenged and may be avoided by those who wish to follow what they regard as the implication of Hume's attack on causal necessity. However, the term is used in the language of the layman. Nor has it been abandoned by all inquirers. Thus, I introduce it in order to pursue the discussion in the broadest context possible. Later, after treating different interpretations of the term "cause," I shall rely on a somewhat different language.

[6] I do not intend this term to be taken in a strong sense. "Mechanistic" essentially refers to schemes that require antecedent rather than future conditions which are believed relevant to explanation.

[7] "Teleological" refers to schemes that require either purposes or logically controlling conditions (or both) that do not exist as actual antecedent conditions but which are possibilities that must be identified in an adequate explanation.

istic view that the universe adheres to logic, particularly a logic that either is or is like a deductive argument that concerns relations in which what follows in some sense requires its premises. A causal relation would then be a logical relation in which the effect is necessitated by the cause, much like the conclusion of a syllogism. The way in which a system serves to explain something under this view should be obvious. The system explains one of its elements in the way premises lead to conclusions. In general, this position is illustrated in philosophies such as that of Spinoza or Leibniz.

The view that causes are correlated events derives most directly from Hume. One way of characterizing this view is to formulate its main principle in terms of variations of states or situations. Variations in one situation correspond to variations in another. There is a correlation between observed changes in what is perceived and known. But the correlation is not one of necessity. It is simply observable and for purposes of control, predictable in a gross way. Unlike traditional determinism, the system to which the correlation view appeals is open to deviations from the predicted events. Consequently, the advocate of this interpretation may claim that there is no reason why novelties cannot occur as deviations or variations on the regularities of the world – on the correlations that explanation cites. Thus, this interpretation of "cause" may seem to avoid the determinism of the other interpretations. However, there are reasons, to be indicated below, for claiming its alliance with these. The view deserves particular attention here, because contemporary inquirers are most likely to believe they follow some version of this view. And those who claim that all things can be explained in terms of this kind of cause, or who claim that nothing resists such explanation in principle, must be answered, since they would argue that the other two views are dead, and that their own view may be adequate to explanations of creativity.

Final causes, which are central to teleological explanation, stand in sharp contrast to efficient causes interpreted as correlations. It is well known, too, that teleological explanation and the concept of final cause has been either rejected or looked upon with suspicion in much of Anglo-American literature in this century which is devoted to philosophies of science. However, some writers in the analytic tradition have recently reintroduced the idea of finality in terms of the view that purposive acts as well as behavioral regularities and deviations must be acknowledged in an adequate study of human decision making.[8] Furthermore, the concept

---

[8] Let me say here that one version of teleology to be indicated later is promising as an appropriate system within which creative acts can fit. This is developmental teleology. But this must be developmental teleology that includes gaps and discontinuities within

of final cause has played a role in a tradition in philosophy that is still alive and has gained strength through a growing interest in Hegelian philosophy and German Idealism. In any case, the kind of system characterizable as teleological does appear openly as well as tacitly in contemporary speculation about creativity.[9]

B. THE PARADOX OF CREATIVITY

In turning to a closer look at the relevance of explanation to creativity, it is important to recall what has been said about the way in which the concepts of Novelty Proper and creativity have been established. The presence of Novelty Proper in a creation has been taken as at least phenomenally given. Thus, we began with an acknowledgment that diversity and unexpected structures are at least observed. The insistence on initially accepting what is phenomenally given is necessary in order to determine what is at stake. Even the denial of what appears is an admission that the appearance is a possibility and that it must be characterizable, if only so that it can be denied. However, at this stage of consideration, to deny what is phenomenally given would be to beg the question at hand in favor of determinism. It would be to start inquiry with a ready-made theory that rejects the description of creative activity as the production of what appears as (valuable) Novelty Proper and that construes the observer of creative acts as somehow deluded. The surprise we may experience in believing ourselves to recognize new things would be the result of self-deception and ignorance. But this view must be based on a theory, and it turns on an issue that is not confined to what is observed. The issue concerns how to interpret what is observed, and whatever the interpretation, it presupposes some fundamental metaphysical commitment.

In the light of the above account of explanation, we can now ask, Is it possible to subject spontaneity to explanation while rejecting the interpre-

---

what develops. It must admit singular actions and singular directions and aims. Thus, it is not wholly conceptual. At least some of the final causes must be generated autonomously. In such a system, explanations of individual instances of creation would include *post hoc* descriptions of correlations. But these would be limited and could not be exhausted by links between instances of Novelty Proper and previous processes. Such explanations would be something like partial explanations in history in which unique events (human actions) are traced to other unique events in the past.

[9] In an essay unfortunately overlooked by most inquirers into creativity, C. S. Peirce argues that teleological as well as mechanistic views are forms of necessitarianism. Necessitarianism is the denial of spontaneity. See "The Doctrine of Necessity Examined," *Collected Papers of Charles Sanders Peirce,* edited by Charles Hartschorne and Paul Weiss (Cambridge, Massachusetts: Harvard University Press, 1935), Vol. VI, Paragraphs 36-65.

tation of it as illusory? Is there a form of explanation that can embrace the tension between spontaneity and orderliness and intelligibility in creative activity? Such explanation is possible, but with the proviso that the explanation is not only incomplete but also inclusive of an increment of paradox.

The claim that there is a paradox inherent in spontaneity can be sharpened by showing that those who wish to understand it rationally without implying its denial either tacitly or openly appeal to an element of unintelligibility in their categories of explanation. For purposes of illustration, I shall consider first that part of Whitehead's theory of reality which is concerned with the creative self-determination of process. Whitehead's approach is chosen because he adopts one form of rationalism that aims at making all things intelligible in terms of categories. At the same time, he affirms the reality of spontaneity. The theory, then, is of particular interest for bringing into relief the paradoxical nature of creativity.[10]

1. Whitehead and Explanation

As already suggested, an explanation must provide a statement of one or more categories or principles in a system of connections under which the occurrence of novelty can be subsumed. However, if the system is to include novelty, it must contain at least one principle that does not reduce what is new to what is old. The account cannot imply the equivalence of novelty with data (laws, conditions, and circumstances) that existed before its occurrence. Thus the explanation must, as Whitehead's does, assume a principle of creativity, a principle affirming that what is new is not completely derivable from the data existing prior to the creative act.

To assume a general principle of creativity is not, however, to determine the origin of novelty. The assumption simply tells us that novelty appears in certain processes. The principle is not, then, an operative principle but a generalization that novelties are claimed to occur. And what is further required of such an explanation is a specification of the factors responsible for individual exemplifications of creativity.

The way this requirement may be met is suggested by Whitehead's description of the structure discoverable within all acts of self-determination. His analysis offers three components necessary to any creative

---

[10] There are, to be sure, other studies of process or change that might have been selected. However, no writer, I believe, has, while insisting on the ineradicable and fundamental character of creativity, sought a more thoroughly rational account of the phenomenon than has Whitehead.

process. These three constituents are: subjective form (the way the process develops the data available to it), subjective aim (the goal or purpose that "lures" the self-determination of the process), and the subject (the unity of the process).[11]

Whatever may condition an event, those conditions are effective in a unique way in accordance with the three essential features of process. Thus, each creative process is autonomous with respect to its conditions. Neither its structure nor its character can be fixed until it is complete. For change is integral to the nature of the outcome. As Whitehead says, "... *how* an actual entity becomes constitutes *what* that actual entity is. ... Its being is constituted by its 'becoming.'" [12]

It follows, then, that subjective form and subjective aim develop throughout the act of self-determination. Thus, Whitehead tells us that the subjective aim of an actual entity is "gradually shaped in the process itself." [13] And just as the aim – that which functions as a lure guiding the subject and its subjective form – undergoes evolution, so does the subjective form.[14]

Whitehead's insistence on the role of change in determining the nature of a process is consistent with what other writers consider a cardinal feature of creativity in art – that the artist does not know until he has said it exactly what it is he wants to say or how he shall say it.[15] If he did, he would have already created. But the artist does not proceed according to a finished plan as he works with his materials. The plan takes shape as the creator encounters the resistance and demands of the medium. Conse-

---

[11] References to the factors present in an actual entity are included in Whitehead's list of categories of explanation, in *Process and Reality* (New York: Social Science Book Store, 1941), pp. 33-39. However, my statements are derived from explanatory comments scattered throughout this work as well as *Adventures of Ideas* (New York: Macmillan, 1933). Subsequent references will be abbreviated as PR for *Process and Reality* and AI for *Adventures of Ideas*. It is only fair to observe that I am, of course, oversimplifying Whitehead's theory. But my purpose is not to give an exposition, but rather to focus on those points which are most crucial in the kind of analytical description that seeks to impose rationality on the creative process. In this connection, it must be added that the discussion of Whitehead may not do justice to the import of his total philosophy or to his most fundamental conclusions about the character of creativity. But, again, my purpose is not to interpret Whitehead, but rather to illustrate my point by considering one part of his theory in which he specifies explanatory principles or factors that include internal limits on the explicability of creativity.

[12] PR, pp. 34-35.

[13] PR, p. 323.

[14] AI, p. 328. Whitehead indicates here that the valuating activity of a process modifies its subjective form.

[15] This point is the basis for A. C. Bradley's well-known distinction between subject and substance in poetry. And the statement occurs explicitly in Samuel Alexander, *Art and the Material*, The Adamson Lecture for 1925 (New York: Longmans, 1925), pp. 11-12. See also Eliseo Vivas, particularly "Naturalism and Creativity," *Creation and Discovery, Essays in Criticism and Aesthetics* (New York: Noonday Press, 1955), p. 154.

quently, it is not implausible to say, as Whitehead indicates, that all creative activity involves a gradual transformation of the purpose and structure of the act according to the intrinsic and extrinsic exigences of self-development. However, granted that Whitehead's analysis seems to do justice to creative change, the question remains: Which one of the components discovered by the analysis is the primary source of control that effects novelty?

Neither subjective form nor subjective aim can be the condition sought. Subjective form cannot be the primary source of novelty, because as Whitehead recognizes, it is modified by the evaluating activity of the process. Thus, subjective form is more like an effect than a cause; it is that which expresses the control in the process. Subjective aim cannot originate novelty, for even if an aim could function as an agency or originator of change, it is nevertheless something that is proposed for a subject. And it is the subject that is responsible for realizing the ideal. The ideal awaits realization; it cannot realize itself.

But most important for showing that the subjective aim cannot effect spontaneity is the fact that the ideal proposed for the subject, as indicated above, changes throughout the creative act. Indeed, a distinction must be made between the initial and the final subjective aim. On the one hand, the final purpose, as Whitehead recognizes, does not exist until the process is complete. If it did, the resultant synthesis would not be novel, for its total structure as governed by the aim would already have been given in the envisaged ideal. On the other hand, the initial purpose cannot be the same once the creative act progresses beyond its first stage. Consequently, if the aim is not determinate, but is rather incomplete during the act of creation, it could not be the primary agency of novelty.

The agency responsible for creativity must lie in the autonomous subject or unity of the process. And this conclusion is affirmed by Whitehead. He tells us, "The regulative principle is derived from the novel unity which is imposed on them by the novel creature in process of constitution. Thus the immediate occasion from the spontaneity of its own essence must supply the missing determination for the synthesis of subjective forms." [16]

This conclusion does tell us which one of the three factors must be primarily responsible for originality. Yet it does not provide us with an explanation that makes creativity fully rational. The difficulty is not simply that the word "spontaneity" does not refer to an explanatory

---

[16] AI, p. 328.

principle. For the problem, to repeat, is to discover the agency or basic conditions from which novelty comes. As the source of novelty, such conditions contain within them all the requisites for a radical leap to that which is not traceable to the old. To characterize the source of novelty as a "creative" agency or as that which is "spontaneous" seems necessary in order that the analysis avoid denying the fact of novelty. The difficulty under consideration, then, does not lie in the objection that the appeal to "spontaneity" is question begging, but rather lies in the paradoxical nature of that which conditions novelty – in the principle of spontaneity itself, whatever may be its locus in the creative process. It is this paradox that must next be examined.

Since the object of the creative process does not have a determinate unity until it is complete, it follows that the essence or unity by virtue of which there is a subject in process cannot be fixed. The subject must determine itself throughout the change. It has no determinate being until the process is actualized. Formulated in terms of human activity, the point is that during the creative act the creator is not fully determined. He is not determined because he is in the act of developing toward what he will be in the future, what he will be once the process attains synthesis in the object to be created. Thus Whitehead says that it is the subject-superject – the initial essence and the future essence of the process, each ingredient in the other – that effects self-determination. It is the artist as a person to be in the future as well as the person in the present who is responsible for the creative act. But the future artist does not yet exist. Only the present artist, whose consciousness is a product of past and present conditions, exists. Thus, the creating agency – the source which can, if anything can, be held responsible for Novelty Proper – is at its core disrupted. In short, the essence of the agent of spontaneity does not have determinate being: it is not a unity. The creating agent – the agent in its capacity as creating – is nothing, i.e., the agent as source of spontaneity or as spontaneity itself, does not constitute an intelligible datum. Insofar as it is a source of spontaneity, it exhibits no structure.

This paradox, it should be emphasized, is not that the creator is in part determined by the future which does not exist. The telic character of the creative process is granted. The point is that in telic processes which yield Novelty Proper, the future, is of a special kind. It is not yet determined and thus, for the creative agent, has neither existence nor a predetermined subsistent being. It is not a determinate possibility. By contrast, a teleological process which is not creative is not subject to the arationality suggested here. A seed developing into a plant, for example, may be said to have a predetermined future awaiting realization. But in this case, the agency of change has a unity inherent within its structure.

Thus, it must be emphasized once more that the issue is not confined to the problem of accounting for change. The paradox in question is to be found not in every instance of change, but rather in events yielding Novelty Proper – in events in which change is not structured according to predetermined results. It is in activities which change and are spontaneous that the paradox is found.

2. The Paradox in the Context of the Husserlian Account of Consciousness

This paradox may perhaps be brought into sharper relief when it is formulated within the framework of Husserl's conception of the nature of consciousness as intentional. If consciousness occurs, it must do so insofar as it is of or about an object. And the filling out of consciousness, the structure and unity of consciousness, is dependent upon its confrontation of structure and unity in the object. The creator's consciousness, then, like any consciousness, can have determinate being only insofar as it intends an object.

Yet creating-consciousness must be directed toward an object given in the future to be created. But the created future, as distinct from a non-created or predetermined future, does not yet subsist for creating-consciousness. That is to say, the unity of the created object is not present to creating-consciousness. The unity is given only to created-consciousness. Thus creating-consciousness at its core has no unity, no essence. Creating-consciousness is empty, or more accurately, is not a determinate thing. For while the structure of the creator's consciousness may have the general character of trying-to-intend-something-new, the essence of consciousness as creating that newness is not given. It does not, until finished, intend the newness, for it does not yet have an object to intend for itself.

3. Nicolai Hartmann's Acknowledgement of the Radical Puzzle

It will be enlightening at this point to pursue the paradox of creativity in the context of the phenomenological approach suggested by Nicolai Hartmann. For although Hartmann's theory is like Whitehead's in accepting the actuality of spontaneity, it attempts to explain the phenomenon along different lines: and in doing so, it too leads to an element of arationality in spontaneity.

Hartmann's phenomenology of experience leads to an ontology that calls for a stratification of reality.[17] It is not necessary to adopt in its entirety Hartmann's scheme and terminology. But it is necessary to focus on the two strata he considers crucial in his analysis of values. Granted that reality has the kind of structure suggested by Hartmann, creating-consciousness or, more generally, the creative agent, may be considered as functioning in relation to two levels of determination. The more elementary level consists in "actual being," that sphere of reality which can be empirically known and which is governed by efficient causality. Each component of this stratum is understood in relation to a network of other actual components which comprise its conditions and effects. And its intelligibility is dependent upon the possibility of subsuming it under natural causal laws and assigning it conditions present within the network.

In so far as creating-consciousness exists at this level, it is an effect traceable to prior conditions such as those of the environment, past experiences, available methods of operation and materials, etc. But actual being does not exhaust the reality of creating-consciousness. For creating-consciousness is valuational and is directed by ideals not yet actual. Values not given in the causal network are operative in bringing about the results marked as novel. Thus, creating-consciousness also functions at the second level of reality, "ideal being." [18]

Ideal being is dependent upon the first stratum, which is its necessary condition. Yet it is governed by its own teleological laws and its own final causes. As such, it is autonomous with respect to actual being. And insofar as creating-consciousness functions at this level, it is autonomous and must be understood in terms of the ideals it discerns within the higher stratum.

It is important to notice that this conception of creating-consciousness differs from Whitehead's. Ignoring the difference between their general positions, what is important for our purposes is that, for Hartmann, creating-consciousness, unlike Whitehead's subjective unity, is subject to the stratification that pervades reality. Thus, the creative activity of consciousness is possible because consciousness functions in more than one realm of determination. Creativity, like freedom, is a relationship between strata of reality – between the strata of efficient and final causality. The oper-

---

[17] An exposition and explanation of the stratification of being in its relation to human consciousness is found in Hartmann's *Ethics,* translated by Stanton Coit (New York: Macmillan, 1932), in particular, Volumes I and III.
[18] Although Hartmann's discussion turns on a conception of values, the argument holds even if we retain neutrality about the addition of value to Novelty Proper in creations. What is at issue concerns "ideal being" or a domain of possibility relative to actual "facts."

ation of teleological determination makes possible the occurrence of components of reality that are new in relation to the network of mechanistic determination. And the presence of mechanistic determination makes possible the actualization of ends given teleologically.

Whatever may be said about the adeqaucy of this theory as an ontology, what is important here is that Hartmann's approach does not make spontaneity amenable to the requirements of rationality. That it does not can be seen in the way in which the theory demands that novelty be related to reality. Within its own stratum, the result of a process must be understood in terms of the laws of that sphere. Hence, a "new" result is not new in relation to its own stratum. It can be considered new only as a component of a higher stratum which is novel in relation to the lower. It must, then, share its novelty with the total network of determination to which it belongs. And the issue concerning the origin of novelty has shifted from a consideration of spontaneity in individual processes to the problems of the "emergence" of strata.

The extent to which creativity can be made rational, then, depends upon the extent to which "emergence" is an adequate explanatory principle. A thorough treatment of the issue in this form would require consideration of the controversy over emergence. In this connection, it must be observed that, for science as generally interpreted – as assuming the pervasiveness of a network of causal connections or regularities which it is the task of science to discover – emergence either must be denied, or if admitted, interpreted so as to conform to the criteria of scientific explanation. On the first alternative, novelty, along with emergence, would be denied. On the second alternative, emergence cannot conform to science so long as predictability is necessary for explanation. But "emergence" refers to qualities that are unpredictable on the basis of a set of data, a logic, an accepted theory, and an appropriate hypothesis.[19]

Thus, whatever the interpretation called for by science, "emergence," like "spontaneity," serves at present to name but not explain the gap between causal conditions and the "new phenomenon." [20] "Emergence" means that knowledge is insufficient for predicting a set of characteristics.

---

[19] In Paul Henle's article, cited above, Henle argues that "emergence" refers to the unpredictability of a quality on the basis of known causes. A basis for this interpretation is present in the work of Lloyd Morgan, who was one of the key writers responsible for the concept of emergence in the literature of this century. See especially *The Emergence of Novelty, op. cit.*

[20] See Eliseo Vivas, *The Moral Life and the Ethical Life* (Chicago: University of Chicago Press, 1950), 150-155. Vivas contends that the term "emergence" obfuscates the issue concerning the attempt to distinguish reality into levels as a "Crypto-emergence" theory; and this is a label that seems to apply to Hartmann.

And if "emergence" is simply a cover for ignorance, its application to the phenomenon of spontaneity leaves open the question whether creativity is arational.

However, the theory of the stratification of reality, as Hartmann recognizes, does not claim that what occurs at a higher level of determination is explained by the concept of "emergence." The theory is simply a description of the structure of reality. It tells us that reality is not structured by continuity; rather, it is discontinuous.

Moreover, further description of the relationship between the two strata would not reveal continuity. Rather, complete rational understanding of the creative process is denied. Hartmann admits that there is an arational element in his scheme. He sees this arationality in human consciousness – in that being which somehow links the mechanistic and teleological strata. Since human consciousness functions in both realms, its character and activity in the mechanistic sphere is in part conditioned by the telic level. Accordingly, human consciousness acts as a mediator between the two strata. Thus, human consciousness has a "double nature"; it has being in "an entity having two strata." [21] And in regard to the form of the unity of these determinations in one being, Hartmann says,

> To grasp this peculiarity in its structure transcends the limits of human understanding – just as, in every possible conception of the moral freedom of the person, there remains something wholly irrational. Just this unity, nevertheless, the personal essence, is something which cannot be resolved into its constituents; it is a categorical novelty, an irrational remainder.[22]

The paradox, then, lies in the insistence upon the distinction between strata, set over against the autonomy and unity of the subject or agency which brings novelty into real being. The autonomous agency loses autonomy insofar as it functions at either or both levels. Or, if it maintains its autonomy and unity, it fails to have continuity with either level, and it thereby ceases to be real in a way that is rational.

It is important to notice that by viewing novelty as residing in the difference between two strata, creativity consists in the discovery and actualization of ideals already having being. A value, then, cannot be construed as a new value, but only as a formerly unknown and unactualized value. To conceive of values as radically new – new in relation to themselves within their own level of determination – would be to introduce a second "irrational remainder," a second discontinuity within the

---

[21] Hartmann, *Ethics,* Vol. I, p. 268.
[22] *Ibid.,* p. 269.

agency of spontaneity, and a gap within strands of teleological being. This second discontinuity would mark a break in the laws of determination of the teleological stratum. If such a break were not possible, the creating subject could not effect novelty and could be autonomous only as a mediator. In order that it be autonomous and spontaneous, it must negate both mechanistic and teleological determination.[23] But since a creating agency would be responsible for originating something not given in the telic network, its essence as mechanistically and teleologically determined would be disrupted. It would be non-continuous, lacking in unity; and precisely at the crucial point of creative determination, it would not be intelligible.

The main contention of this section has been that paradox is encountered by those who attempt to give a rational account of the origin of novelty without insisting on its reduction to continuities. It is now appropriate to consider the implications of those approaches which explicitly or implicitly deny the reality of radical novelty in order to avoid the paradox; for it might be claimed that if spontaneity is both paradoxical and arational, and if the world is rational, the notion that there is spontaneity must be excluded from our thought about the world. In short, if spontaneity appears to be arational, then it can be only an appearance and not a real ingredient in the world. In considering this alternative I shall attempt to show that the contradictory view encounters difficulties which point to an arational remainder – a paradox at least as fundamental as the paradox of spontaneity.

C. THE REALITY OF SPONTANEITY AND THE CHALLENGE OF DETERMINISM

It must be emphasized once more that the kind of newness in question is not that which is attributable to a first occurrence of an experience. No one but a Parmenidean, perhaps, would deny this kind of novelty. As was indicated at the outset, the kind of novelty in question is that which appears in such a way as to be the mark of something different in type or kind, even though the act of experiencing this difference may be singular. The novelty-characteristic presents itself as a new structure exemplifying Form, not a new thing with an old structure. But an inquirer who refuses to relinquish a rationalistic and deterministic perspective will insist that at most, only immediate, subjective experiences and things in their indi-

---

[23] This point is argued by Hartmann in *Ethics,* Vol. III, "Moral Freedom." But since autonomy is described in terms of moral freedom, valuational decisions are acts of selection, not acts yielding novel results.

viduality are unique and that what they are about, or what they are intelligibly related to, can be subjected to explanation in the form of necessities or regularities that remain to be discovered. From this point of view, there could be no radical breaks in the connections among Forms and structures that comprise the world.

As already proposed, most loosely, determinism is a view grounded on the ontological presupposition that all things in the world are predictable. More generally, determinism construes all things as determined in the minimal sense that they are identifiable in contexts such that a change in context in one place is functionally related to a change elsewhere. More strictly, of course, determinism affirms that if we have information about all the particles of the universe at a given time, we could calculate the state of all the particles of the universe at any other time. In the strict form, determinism requires (at least in principle) unlimited accuracy and precision in the calculations that are incorporated into explanations. Further, it purports to offer reversible calculations — statements about the world of the future imply statements about the past, and *vice versa*.

At this point, it is necessary to turn for a moment to an argument for rejecting traditional determinism and the possibility that this rejection offers a basis for defending the view that radical novelty is undeniable. It is now known that certain physical phenomena have not and perhaps cannot be subjected to the precise predictions required by an ideally perfected determinism. In the case of the flow of air around an airplane's wing, for instance, no formula can be given for calculating the movement of air within approximately two inches of the wing. The phenomenon of quantum leaps and the accompanying principle of indeterminacy (or of uncertainty) also illustrates this point.

It is important to notice that we are not referring to acceptable experimental margins of error. The current state of knowledge suggests that the phenomena in question are unpredictable either because of the interference of our instruments of observation or because of something inherent in the phenomena. In any case, the possibility of subjecting all phenomena to explanations that include predictions is ruled out. Does this lend support to a spontaneitist view which affirms radical novelty? I do not think the issue of whether radical novelty is undeniable can be settled by appeal to the unpredictability of quantum leaps. First, it is not unplausible to claim that this unpredictability will be overcome at some time in the future if the state of our knowledge is advanced. I do not mean to make this claim, but it may at least be offered as a possibility. Further, even if unpredictability of quantum leaps cannot be overcome, the issue of radical novelty centers on macroscopic lawfulness, on the appearance of phenomena of an order of observability within which phenomena in general are predictable. What is in question are human acts and their products, and, whether these, like much human behavior, are predictable, regardless of whether microscopic physical phenomena included within such processes are unpredictable.

1. Positivism

Before considering further the deterministic perspectives, additional attention must be given to what I believe is a weaker version of determinism, a view that rejects novelty by excluding it from its sights. The view is what I shall call positivism – a view which is based on the interpretation of explanation as a statement of regularities, and which purports to rely on natural science for its model of understanding.[24] Strictly speaking, positivism ignores the existence of spontaneity. It does so by insisting upon the primacy of observability and predictability as criteria for empirical knowledge. Gustav Bergmann, for instance, speaks of the absence from the world we know of what he refers to as "novelty proper" or "radical novelty," both terms essentially referring to what I described as Novelty Proper. His reason for ruling out radical newness is that its admission would require that the categories and structure within which it occured be impermanent.[25] Presumably, impermanent categories would not furnish knowledge by which extrapolations into the past and the future could be made. Thus, what Bergmann seems to insist upon is that, if the world can be described in terms of what he accepts as positive knowledge, then some degree of constancy must be present in the world. And this is to say that the possibility of positive knowledge depends upon looking at the world in such a way as to emphasize the kind of data that will yield to our "positive" way of looking.

---

[24] The label "positivistic" is used in the broadest sense, for convenience, to include any view that insists on the use of "empirical methods" – the adherence to publicly verifiable data, predictability, etc., as necessary criteria of knowledge – and the "meaninglessness" of assertions that do not abide by its strictures. Most generally, the term "positivism" is used here to cover those views for which causal relations, and all admissible data and principles, are to be understood in terms of correlations. This meaning of the term may meet with objections, but since I am not committed to labels, I would be willing to adjust or abandon the term where this is appropriate.

[25] Gustav Bergmann, op. cit., pp. 209-221. This article presents a rigorous critique of Henle's paper, "The Status of Emergence," op. cit. Bergmann's purpose is to examine historicism and holism in relation to the expectations of scientific theory. But he does discuss the place of novelty in such views, and he emphatically removes from the concerns of scientific inquiry the possibility that radical novelty can occur in time.

The conclusion that the positivistic approach ignores spontaneity and its product, novelty, is explicitly indicated by Russell's account of causality and its relation to the predictability of human behavior. Russell points out that the determinist in science need only foresee the kind of act he hopes to predict. He has little "practial interest" in predicting the "fine shades which cannot be foreseen." [26] The deviations not calculable by inquirers who search for causes in the form of regularities are to be ignored, since such irregularities are irrelevant for the purposes of explanation. One could argue, for example, that predicting an earthquake at a given time and given place would not require foreknowledge of specific qualities of the disturbance. The quake might very well have unique and novel characteristics, but foreknowledge of these characteristics is more than can or should be expected of the prediction. But to disclaim the need for foreseeing individuality in a predicted event is to disclaim an interest in features that are of utmost importance in the kind of events in which novelty and spontaneity occur in their most obvious manifestations, works of art. Indeed, the "fine shades," the minutiae and subtle variations in an aesthetic object are often of such importance as to be the marks of an event that is different in kind or type from any other prior event. It is such variations that "conspire" to exhibit a new structure and thus to newly exemplify a Form. As Croce points out, Don Quixote is a type who possesses some characteristics common to others; yet the Don Quixote type is singular, and, as Don Quixote, is like nothing else in the world.

If the positivist's approach is willing to grant that there is novelty in the world, it is hard to see how novelty could be subjected to the positivistic program for rational understanding. Positive knowledge must look for repeated and repeatable patterns in observations. Its methods call for treating the world in terms of kinds and classes of previously known, observable events.

Moreover, even if the positivist program were capable of describing and predicting in detail unrepeatable or unique events, it should be pointed out that such a prediction would include foreknowledge of the characteristics of the event predicted. If, on the basis of certain data, a logic, a hypothesis, and a theory, something "new" is predicted, that "newness" must be referred to in the prediction statement – the "newness" must be already known. And to the extent that it is already known either it is not "new," or, if it is new, it is a creation achieved by the predictor, in which case, explanation of novelty is complete only if the prediction could have

---

[26] *Our Knowledge of the External World* (London: Allen & Unwin, 1952), p. 234.

been predicted – and so on *ad infinitum,* unless foreknowledge is attributed, ultimately, to an omniscient being.[27]

Thus, the positivist interpretation of the world either must deny in the sense of ignoring the phenomenon in question, or it must openly exclude radical novelty because it presupposes the predictability of all characteristics of reality. On the former alternative, its approach is not relevant to the question whether spontaneity is arational. On the latter alternative, positivism is at bottom a version of the second approach to be considered: the view that denies the reality of novelty by interpreting the appearance of novelty as illusory or deceptive. Consequently, insofar as positivism is concerned with the question of the reality of radical creativity, it can be approached in the way determinism can.

The denial of radical novelty may be openly professed or it may be implied. In either case, the denial depends on the adoption of a version of strict determinism. Earlier, determinism was distinguished into two types: teleological and mechanistic. It is necessary now to examine each of these in turn.

2. *Teleological Determinism*

A teleology may be thought of as answering the question, Why? The answer to this question in psychological contexts would concern certain motives or dispositions to act which, though present prior to the activity to be explained, are directed toward a goal or end which in some sense is responsible as a condition for the direction and development of the disposition to action. In more general extra-psychological as well as psychological contexts, an answer would specify a potentiality or disposition to development toward a definite state that fulfills this development. A final cause functions as a telos or directing principle which is either identical with or grounded in an end that gives direction to a course of events and a series of things which are thought to be explained by the end. In contrast to mechanistic explanation, it is the end to be reached in the future that serves explanation. Nevertheless, whatever distinctions one may make between such a system and mechanistic determinism, both determinisms share a basic commitment to fitting what is to be explained into an ordered scheme that requires the things and events to be explained. Even though the teleologist directs us to future developments rather than ante-

[27] Bergson presents a forceful argument which makes this kind of point against those who believe prediction of novelty is possible. See his *The Creative Mind,* translated by Mabelle L. Andison (New York: Greenwood Press, 1946), especially the section on the Possible and the Real.

cedent conditions, these developments are rational and explanatory because of the necessity by which they are brought about.

It was suggested earlier that teleological determinism requires that instances of novelty are appearances ideally traceable to necessities. Novelty is the mark of difference; but, like every other component and link within the system, difference has a necessary place in a world that changes according to an underlying order, an order that functions in terms of the past or the future. It should be obvious that this expectation excludes the possibility that there is radical novelty in the world. Successful explanation according to this view would find a place for Novelty Proper in a context of ordered connections.

It might be objected that an Hegelian system is teleological and that it nevertheless affirms both evolutionary change and novelty. I shall respond to this objection only briefly, for if the objection is based on an adequate interpretation of Hegel, such a system is not here at issue. Thus, if Hegel's view does not deny novelty in the way I have suggested teleological systems do, then his system cannot be closed. It must be one in which future changes include features not necessitated by potentially or logically operative causes or conditions, or with necessitated stages, within the system as a whole. In such a system, a process and what it constitutes, or a stage and what it leads to, could be otherwise than whatever it happens to be. In any case, I do not wish to claim that all teleological explanations necessarily exclude radical novelty. But, I do wish to claim this of any teleological view that requires a complex of necessities comprising a complete system.

Whether or not an Hegelian or any other version of teleology accepts spontaneity, some teleological views are expressly deterministic. Brand Blanshard, for instance, has taken creativity into account within his own teleology, and he says explicitly that creative acts are controlled by necessities that have their ground in an underlying order not immediately evident to the creator – or to those who look for observable data in trying to understand creativity.[28]

If teleological systems do call for understanding all occurrences in terms of ideal orders, then they are like mechanistic determinisms in aiming at explanations that relegate apparent discontinuity and newness to the level of what has not yet been explained. I shall discuss reasons for rejecting this perspective in connection with the mechanistic approach.

---

[28] *Op. cit.*, Chapters XXI-XXIV.

3. Mechanistic Determinism

Unlike positivism, mechanistic determinism does not limit itself to identifying correlations and regularities (though these may be included in its conceptualization). Its aim is to set forth a system in which laws and fundamental productive conditions explain events, including human behavior. With respect to understanding human behavior, theories of this kind may make central a theory of consciousness or a theory focused on the subject of consciousness. Depending upon which is of primary focus, consciousness may be called "mistaken" in every instance in which it is aware of a phenomenon as novel; or the object of consciousness may be called "unreal," or in some way deficient in being. The former view may rely on a comprehensive theory of physiological, genetic, and environmental conditions of conscious activity, but at some point, it necessarily views consciousness as at least provisionally misled in responding to newness as something irreducible to the past.[29] The latter view is represented in all metaphysical determinisms.

In discussing these approaches, I shall focus attention on psychological determinism. A complete metaphysical theory that is to deny the reality of novelty cannot avoid psychological as well as epistemological considerations, since even if the "illusory" phenomenon is deficient in being, an explanation must be given concerning why consciousness is mistaken or ignorant of the deficiency. Thus, the metaphysical approach must account for the conditions effecting error in consciousness as well as the conditions effecting the occurrence of the appearance. Moreover, if both approaches (that directed toward the object and that directed toward consciousness) are drawn out to completion, their deterministic schemes must encompass both consciousness and its object. Hence, the peculiar difficulty for determinism which, I shall suggest, implies an arationality in its own program, can be treated by beginning with either approach. And since current notions about illusions are psychologically oriented, it will be easier to center on determinism as it is directed toward consciousness.

One of the plainest examples of the psychological approach is that of Freudian psychoanalytic theory.[30] Before looking at Freudian determin-

---

[29] Recent examples include Arthur Koestler's rich but ultimately reductionist interpretation of the creative act in *The Act of Creation* (New York: The Macmillan Company, 1964) as well as B. F. Skinner's behaviorism which recently has been applied to the interpretation of the poet as a creator (*op. cit.*). Koestler and Skinner both view the creator as a product of genetic and environmental conditioning.

[30] Granted that there are other forms of psychoanalytic psychology, so varied as to include "existential psychoanalysis," as well as neo-Freudian and non-Freudian theories,

ism, however, it is only fair to note that the adherents of psychoanalytic theory may not care to deny categorically the reality of novelty. Indeed, I think they must not, if they are to make the practice of psychoanalysis consistent with their theoretical conclusions; for psycho-therapy demands "new" ways of structuring the mind. Freud himself seems inclined toward the admission of a creative, and thus novel transformation of mental life when he speaks of the artist's "mysterious" way of changing desire into acceptable aesthetic form.[31] Nevertheless, Freud's psychoanalytic program depends upon the hope of fully explaining all human behavior. Furthermore, there is a general tendency to interpret psychoanalytic theory as fully deterministic, at least in its aims, and there is sufficient truth in this tendency to warrant using psychoanalytic theory as an example of determinism.

Within the framework of Freudian theory, a phenomenon which is interpreted as illusory presumably can be traced to its origin in the personal or private dynamism of the psyche. Hallucinations experienced in a case of hysteria are interpreted as illusory because they are products of some form of mental conflict that manifests itself in a way peculiar to the person. That a hallucination appears is not denied. But the appearance is characterizable as illusory because it can be described as causally related to other antecedent experiences. And when felt and described by the person suffering from it, it ceases (or should cease) to appear. Knowledge of the origin of the hallucination not only "corrects" the initial interpretation of the appearance as externally caused but it also leads to the extinguishing of the phenomenon entirely. Can an appearance of novelty, then, be described in terms of antecedent experiences so that the appearance vanishes?

In considering this question, it is important to notice that novelty, unlike hallucinations, appears for a kind of consciousness which, though perhaps abnormal in its sensitivity and freedom from stereotyped, hardened patterns of activity, is not pathological. Thus, novelty in general (not specific cases of pathological delusions) need not vanish before the knowing eye of the psychoanalyst and the insights of a patient. If novelty is a "normal" illusion (common to nonpathological consciousness), it may continue to appear as always, even though it is recognized for what it is – a phenomenon the conditions for which are fully known. A "normal"

---

the concern here is with the kind of determinism that calls for interpreting novelty in terms of pre-existing mental contents and drives.

[31] "The Relation of the Poet to Day-Dreaming," *Collected Papers,* Vol. IV translated by Joan Riviere (London: Hogarth Press, 1925), p. 183. See also in *Collected Papers,* V, 222, the first sentence of Freud's essay on Dostoevski: "Before the problem of the creative artist analysis must, alas, lay down its arms."

illusion such as a mirage may be called "illusory" insofar as it is inadequately or mistakenly interpreted. It remains illusory only for the unenlightened. For the enlightened, the phenomenon, though it still appears in its original guise, is not an illusion, since it is not misinterpreted; it is known for what it is. Hence, a mirage of an oasis, if understood, is not sought as source of comfort.

However, whether novelty is construed as abnormal or normal, it has a peculiarity not present in other illusory appearances. Other phenomena called "illusory" appear as like what they are not. They are (with a possible exception that will be separately dealt with) characterized by resemblances to the phenomena of which they are illusions. Ordinary illusions appear as images of things, or as composite images of qualities, antecedently known. For example: a mirage presents itself as that which it is not; and it is a deception by virtue of qualities that it has in common with what it is not and thus with what is already known. A distorted mirror image in a "fun house" (whether or not mistakenly interpreted) is a composite of the exaggeration of qualities already known. And a hallucination such as a specter is a composite or combination of qualities – vapor and flame, or a deceased body and light, for instance – that are otherwise known.

Appearances of novelty on the other hand, are unlike rather than like what is. They cannot, as initially given, be characterized by resemblances to antecedent phenomena. If they could be, they would not even be appearances of novelty; they would not present themselves as instances of novelty.

Now to interpret newness as illusory in the way other appearances are illusory is to construe all appearances of newness as like what they are not. But since there is nothing which they appear to be like but are not, they must be either illusions of nothing or pretenses for nothing but themselves. Hence, if they are illusions of nothing they are not illusions; and if they are deceptions of themselves, they continue to insist on being what they are – appearances of newness.

It might be argued that there are some "illusory" appearances, such as the distorted mirror image, which are initially perceived as unlike rather than like what is. For even if the image is a composite of antecedent qualities, it appears as a "new" thing and thus has the characteristic of novelty: difference in kind. Thus, it may be said, there is no phenomenon independent of the mirror image which the image resembles. And if the image can be shown to be an illusion, then at least one appearance of novelty has been shown to be illusory.

But what is involved in accounting for "illusory" appearances of this sort brings into focus the arationality determinism faces in treating novelty. The account suggested for illusions which, like that of the distorted mirror image, are not traceable to antecedent appearances, presumably accepts the phenomenal objectivity of novelty. For it asserts that the image is radically different and is thus different in type from all prior appearances. Thus, the image is a new identity – a novel structure. Far from denying the phenomenal presence of novelty in the world, this account of "illusory" images affirms it. What, then, could be meant by saying that the phenomenon is "illusory"?

The appearance of novelty cannot be an illusion in the sense of an appearance about which consciousness is deluded or guilty of misinterpretation. This is not to claim that mistakes are never made about instances of novelty. Obviously, someone may fail to recognize novelty because of inflexible ways of seeing or because of some form of blindness. And someone might, because he is ignorant or has forgotten, mistakenly apprehend novelty where there is none. One might, for example wrongly regard a mirror distortion as "new," because of ignorance that the same kind of distortion (the same exaggerated shapes in the same size frame) was to be found long ago in the first "fun house." Or one might mistakenly see a painting by a magazine illustrator as novel, not recognizing that the painting is a composite imitation of some event or persons previously photographed. But in both cases, what leads to error is the limitation on the observer's consciousness of a particular case. The appearance nevertheless presents itself as novelty. And consciousness could be mistaken about the particular case only if the instance, as initially given, is a "novelty-presentation." Thus, that there are, in principle, appearances of novelty in the world cannot be an illusion about which consciousness is deluded.

Hence, the only meaning that can be given to interpreting newness as illusory in principle is that all instances of novelty-presentations can be given a locus in a total determinstic network. And in order that the appearance of Novelty Proper be accounted for, each instance of it must be traced to other elements in the scheme.

What would be the consequences of successful accomplishment of this task? Suppose that the account "corrects" the deficiency of knowledge that leads consciousness to regard the initial presentation as new. Perhaps the answer is that the initial presentation would then vanish, much as hallucinations are said to vanish under psychoanalysis. But more likely, the answer will be offered that the deterministic account would not affect consciousness in such a way that the initial appearance must vanish. Is it possible that the thing explained could continue to seem new? But how could we construe as novel something which is known in all its connections within a system? The thing could only be new in the sense that it is a singular, a unique individual, as well as a particular thing with a place in a system of connections. Its novelty could only be its singularity, its existence in one and only one place in the system. This kind of novelty turns out to be numerical novelty. At most, the thing would be new in the sense that all things are different from one another by virtue of holding one place in time and in the totality of things in an ordered complex. This is the way in which we might regard a recently identified virus within a larger complex of organic and non-organic things, if we knew all its properties and relations to other things. To be a "new kind of virus" could only mean "to be a recently understood virus." At bottom, then, Novelty Proper is rejected by both accounts of the consequences of a successful deterministic explanation.

There is, however, a crucial problem that remains, whether one claims that novelty vanishes altogether or that it would not vanish but would be modified and regarded as novelty of singularity. The theorist who is committed to determinism would need to show how consciousness can be transformed so as to cope with and eradicate a presentation the being of which was initially cut off from connections with the deterministic scheme. The recent discovery of the virus would require a transformation of biological knowledge. How can the determinist account for this change? Such a transformation of consciousness is itself an appearance of novelty – an appearance that the theorist must either grant to be outside of his determinism or accept as an illusion demanding explanation by his theory. And if he were successfully to turn his theoretical sights upon this illusion, he would once more be faced with the need for reflecting upon his own transformation of consciousness – the novelty-presentation he would effect – as he discovered the place of the first transformation in his deterministic network. And I submit that this reflective process would be required *ad infinitum,* unless the theory broke with its deterministic presuppositions and assumed a principle of creativity, in which case the arationality would be given a locus in the principle itself.

This problem can be seen from a broader perspective. First, it must be observed that the deterministic account would need to include knowledge of the relationship between the appearance in its presentation as novelty and the appearance as understood within the deterministic network. Thus the deterministic network must somehow be enlarged so that it can provide reasons why consciousness, if it had access to a perfect understanding of the necessary links between novelty-presentations and the world, could be "corrected," not bound by finite perspectives from which things are discovered and appear surprising. Intelligence would need to understand its own function within the deterministic chain operative in the world. If determinism could provide such understanding, it assumes a position which, after all, does call for extinguishing appearances of novelty. And it assumes this position in a special way. It assumes a comprehension that transcends intelligence as a finite component within the world, i.e., as an existent which is limited and subject to historical conditions. Transcendent, deterministic consciousness, in understanding existential consciousness, could not be deluded by appearances. It could not be deluded, because it would need to assume the posture of omniscience. Thus, only if man could become God could he successfully deny or explain the phenomenal reality of novelty.

This point about the implication of the deterministic approach to spontaneity can be suggested by an analogy in which the determinist is pictured with a book of knowledge in which each event is described in terms of fixed laws and is given a locus within a total network of all events, past, present, and future. The determinist finds himself as well as all other consciousnesses described in the book. He sees within the book that his existential consciousness is confronted with "novelty-presentations." And his transcendent consciousness understands why these appearances occur within the world as they do and why his existential consciousness grasps them as appearances of novelty. But his transcendent understanding could not change by one iota either the novelty-presentation or existential consciousness. They occur independently of his knowledge. If they did not, if transcendent consciousness intervened, the determinist chain would be broken. If the determinist could change the book, the book would be wrong. That is, the book would not exhaustively treat all factors operative in the causal chain. For if transcendent consciousness did change the book just once, the book cannot guarantee that what it says now may not be different according to the whim – the spontaneous whim – of the determinist in his position of transcendence. But if deterministic understanding must accept novelty-presentations as given within necessary continuities in the world, there would remain a radical gap between the transcendent, deterministic consciousness and the existential, determined consciousness. The gap would lie between perfect intelligence, not surprised or deluded, and finite intelligence surprised by what appear to be occasional radical changes in the world. And spontaneity as an actual ingredient of the world is denied for the sake of accepting an arationality in the relation between infinite mind and finite mind, between transcendent being and existential contingency.

Determinism, then, implies puzzles just as fundamental as its opposite. The rationality it attempts to impose on all of reality is limited. This point and the above line of argument in defense of it should be taken into account by those scientists and admirers of a "technology of human behavior" who make such claims as: "Neither view [the prescientific commitment of man's autonomy and the scientific conviction that all man's behavior is determined by genetic endowment and environmental circumstances] can be proved, but it is in the nature of scientific inquiry that the evidence should shift in favor of the second." [32] To affirm that spontaneity is real as well as phenomenally observed – to affirm that appearances of Novelty Proper cannot be explained away or shown to be illusions awaiting more comprehensive knowledge – is no less reasonable, at bottom, than determinism. This point serves as a negative justification of those views that try to make room for radical newness, whether they do so by abandoning all attempts to explain it or by including the acknowledgement of radical newness in one or more categories of a system of explanation.

In concluding this section, let me reiterate that, given what has been traditionally regarded as rational understanding, the theoretical approaches which accept the actuality of spontaneity encounter an element of paradox or arationality that seems to be inherent within the nature of spontaneity. The reason explanation cannot avoid this irrational increment is that the phenomenon of spontaneity is peculiar in that it eludes categories and principles which, in their capacity as being rational, insist upon having unity, even if only in the form of constancy of regularity. They necessarily impose repeatability or continuity on the phenomena which they successfully interpret. Other kinds of change which do not disclose novelty but rather conform to antecedent patterns may not resist continuities. But spontaneity, since it yields newness, does resist.

It was argued that theories that reject this view and deny the actuality of spontaneity must nevertheless come to grips with the appearance of novelty. They must show that the appearance of novelty is in some sense illusory. And the way in which a theory can show this leads, in its own way, once again to perplexities that indicate a paradox inherent in the world.

It is of utmost importance, however, to insist that the arationality for

---

[32] B. F. Skinner, *Beyond Freedom and Dignity* (New York: Alfred A. Knopf, 1971), p. 101.

which I have argued presupposes an acceptance of rationality as it has traditionally been interpreted. Whether or not spontaneity is unintelligible as well as non-rational depends upon whether intelligibility is identified with rationality as traditionally conceived. In this connection, I should like to indicate a way of approaching the problem of making spontaneity intelligible. The concluding section of this chapter will set the stage for Chapter III.

D. INTELLIGIBILITY AND THE RESOURCES OF LANGUAGE

If the issue with which we are concerned is broadened and formulated as a question about how "the arational" in general may be made intelligible, suggestions, of course, can be found in the philosophical tradition – in Plato, Aristotle, Plotinus, Spinoza, etc. However, some contemporary movements have brought the issue into sharp focus, treating it as a major problem requiring resolution or at least clarification as a step toward a reconstituted view of the function of philosophy. More specifically, the proper way to bring lucidity to a mode or level of human reality not amenable to conceptual thought has recently been a crucial concern for personalists, existentialists, and some representatives of Thomistic philosophy, as well as others such as Bergson and perhaps Wittgenstein. It would be inappropriate at this point, however, to attempt a list of names, for my purpose is not to survey the literature but simply, first, to emphasize that the issue is alive, and then to prepare the way for my own approach by mentioning one of the crucial directions possible for a study of the problem. This approach has an affinity with some of the suggestions in Bergson's writing. It will be helpful to consider briefly some of the limitations and merits to be found in what he says.

Whether one agrees or disagrees with his critique of abstract thinking, Bergson's arguments about the limitations of discursive analysis and the need for non-abstractive, non-discursive knowledge cannot be ignored.[33] His advocacy of a kind of intellectual sympathy or intuition points to a way of apprehending an unconceptualizable reality that is in continuous, creative movement. And if the awareness of creative force gained by intuition is immediate and yet intellectual (though not abstractly conceptual), then Bergson's notion of intuition refers to a kind of knowledge that is intelligible without being rational, and it is about something non-

---

[33] Bergson's *Introduction to Metaphysics*, translated by T. E. Hulme (New York: G. P. Putnam's Sons, 1913), of course, deals explicitly with this topic; however, it is to be found in many of Bergson's works. Cf. *The Creative Mind*.

rational which is intelligible. Communication of this knowledge is possible by the use of "fluid concepts." These concepts are of a special order, for they must be appropriate to objects as individualities rather than to continuities abstracted from objects. Thus, the intellectual means to understanding can hardly be called "concepts" in any ordinary sense. They are more like metaphors occurring in poetic language. The language of intuition symbolizes, not directly, but rather indirectly, the reality which intuition makes intelligible for itself.

Bergson's view suggests a way of penetrating what remains a mystery for rational explanation. However, there is a difference between Bergson's notion of the reality which must be intuited and the spontaneity of which I have spoken. For Bergson does not describe the *élan vital* or creative force as paradoxical. It is true that the paradox as I have discussed it appears on the side of conceptual thought. I have tried to show that rationality directed toward spontaneity reaches its limits in the recognition of a conceptual tension. For this reason, I want to insist that spontaneity as it lies beyond the reach of rational understanding is apprehended as paradoxical rather than simply arational. The intelligibility of spontaneity must be found in a kind of apprehension and a kind of language which reflects the structure of this tension.

The emphasis on paradox suggests the need to make spontaneity intelligible in a way that is not quite identical with Bergson's appeal to "fluid concepts" or metaphors in the communication of intuition. Bergson, I think, does not give sufficient importance to the role of conceptualization – to the recognition of Form and structure – in the identification of radical newness. As I have tried to show, Novelty Proper is recognized for what it is in a contrast between, on the one hand, an exhibited structure and exemplified Form, and, on the other hand, past structures and previously exemplified Forms. A conceptual tension grounds the recognition that there are instances of Novelty Proper. However, Bergson's insistence on the role of metaphorical language in giving expression to the apprehension of reality, insofar as it is creative, is especially fruitful. It is this point in Bergson's position that is directly suggestive for the approach I shall propose.[34]

Language is rich in its resources. One of its resources is precision of meaning. The aim of a determinist's view of the world could be expressed by means of this resource. A complete system could be articulated by a

---

[34] The problem of poetry and knowledge has recently been dealt with by many writers. I have tried to clarify the issue in "Art and Symbol," *Review of Metaphysics*, XV, 2 (December, 1961), 256-270.

rigorous language in which every term takes a place in an ordered scheme. But the greater emphasis given to any one resource, the greater the limitations on the variety of other possibilities present in its resources. Thus, a program to construct an ideal, perhaps universal language must sacrifice the richness with which the program starts. As Leibniz illustrates, a universal language requires singularity of meaning for each term in the language. The distinctness of a meaning precludes there being a multiplicity of undetermined meanings. Distinctness and precision may conquer ambiguity and indeterminateness, but subtlety and the power to transform meaning within language as a whole is thereby surrendered. If language is to articulate an understanding of a world in which spontaneity and radical creativity have a place, then it must adopt more than the resource for determinateness and precision in connected meanings. It must rely on other resources as well, including one that ordinarily is thought to stress ambiguity: metaphorical expression.

I should like to suggest that philosophic discourse may join with poetic expression to yield a quasi-conceptual form of language, a language which can in certain ways make intelligible the arational being of spontaneity. As a general recommendation, what I propose is not new. Much philosophical writing long before Bergson has employed a kind of poetic-conceptual way of speaking. Plato's use of myth illustrates a joining of rationally directed dialectic with poetic language – a poetry intended to transcend conceptual thought. But within conceptual argument, philosophers – and, as has been argued by others, scientists, too – have made use of metaphorical expressions that have later been absorbed into philosophical (and scientific) vocabulary: consider the term "power" in "explanatory power," the term "light" which now occurs frequently in expressions such as "throw light on the subject," or the use of the term "clarity" for being precisely evident, or the word "substance" which now means something more than simply "that which stands under." Indeed, the terms "originality" and "spontaneity" are quasi-conceptual, in signifying universally a way of being; but at the same time they lead to an unconceptualizable, non-universal way of being. They can function in this two-fold way to the extent that they are understood through a fusion of conceptual and poetic, or more specifically, metaphorical meaning.

It is significant that some recent philosophers have drawn rather deliberately on poetic or metaphorical expression as an integral part of their discussion of problems which are based upon a notion of a reality that is non-rational and paradoxical. Bergson has already been mentioned. When he speaks of "fluid concepts" or metaphors, he does suggest a way in which language can approach what is beyond concepts, although as indicated above, he does not suggest a way in which intuitions themselves apprehend what is given as rationally paradoxical. However, there is a sense in which Sartre's analysis of consciousness, in contrast to Bergson's, shows how a paradoxical reality can be revealed by language.[35] Sartre's insistence on non-thetic self-consciousness, for instance, points to a structure of consciousness which is peculiar in that, as consciousness, it must be intentional and yet, as self-consciousness, it cannot be intentional of itself as object. Again, the description of consciousness as freedom trapped within being-in-itself suggests a paradox of human reality – a paradox given in the originating, creative function of consciousness. For consciousness is a spontaneity and as such it is what it is not and is not what it is.

How does Sartre's writing illustrate the possibility of communicating and making intelligible a paradoxical, rational being? Sartre employs both conceptual language and poetic or metophorical expression. Along with and within the dialectic of his arguments, Sartre includes metaphorical language. His metaphorical expressions reinforce and enhance his concepts. The term "nothingness," or "naughting," for example, functions in the argument in a metaphorical way to indicate for the reader a being which at bottom cannot be conceptualized. The discussions of anguish and "the look," and the introduction of terms such as "viscous," "bloated," etc., with reference to being-in-itself, function metaphorically to give an immediacy and concreteness to conceptual language. And much of Sartre's literary work, taken as a body, may be considered poetic language which reinforces that rationally structured argument of those works that are thought of as philosophical.

In the next chapter, I shall develop this suggestion about the resources of metaphorical language for the intelligibility of spontaneity. I should like to propose a way of viewing poetic and metaphorical expression that indicates how the apprehension of spontaneity may be clarified and communicated.

---

[35] The following comments on Sartre are based chiefly upon *Being and Nothingness: an Essay on Phenomenological Ontology*, translated by Hazel Barnes (New York: Philosophical Library, 1956), *The Transcendence of the Ego*, translated by Forrest Williams and Robert Kirkpatrick (New York: The Noonday Press, 1957), and his literary works.

CHAPTER III

LANGUAGE AND THE AESTHETIC STRUCTURE OF NOVELTY

INTRODUCTION

The poetic use of language offers a way to further our understanding of radical novelty. But this does not guarantee that poetic language is free of the fundamental problem inherent in the attempt to conceptualize creativity. Poetic language itself may be creative, for it may originate meaning. Thus, it poses the very problem it is intended to clarify. Nonetheless, there are features of poetic language which do illuminate these problems and which point the way to a more comprehensive understanding.

My aim, therefore, is to propose two ways in which poetic language as it is realized in metaphorical expression is especially relevant to the intelligibility of creativity. First, metaphorical expression serves as a way of signifying the unique meanings exhibited in the structures and exemplified Forms that are instances of Novelty Proper. Secondly, metaphorical expression can itself be a way of instancing Novelty Proper. The second function of metaphor is particularly relevant to our purposes, because it offers a model of created objects in which certain fundamental features of Novelty Proper can be sharply delineated.

My plan is to begin by re-examining the difference between creations and non-created productions, here in the specific context of language. I shall first consider the way originative speech transcends familiar speech in broaching what could not otherwise be said in a language that is already established. I shall then consider how creative speech presents new meaning through the articulation of terms that seem to function meaningfully in indirect or oblique ways. With this discussion in mind, I shall turn to a closer examination of the way in which metaphorical expressions refer to and exhibit instances of radical novelty.

A. ORIGINATIVE SPEECH AS OBLIQUE EXPRESSION

The origin of meaning in the evolution of language presents a problem. On the one hand, meanings must be intelligible. They must be understandable, and some of them must be shareable. Those which are both understood and shared must be sufficiently familiar to be recognized and identified by an audience. On the other hand, original meanings are new and initially unfamiliar. It seems, then, that their appearance presents something unintelligible to their audiences. Original meanings are introduced as unrelated to what constituted the world as it was understood before their innovation. Hence, in being productive of novelty, originative speech seems inconsistent with the function of language, that is, with the function of articulating and transmitting identifiable and shared meanings. How is it possible, then, for a speaker to broach meanings that are both intelligible and new?

1. Language and Speech

The term "language" is often used to cover many kinds of activities, from highly complex and abstract oral and written discourse to the simple non-verbal expression of feeling. Accordingly, speech as linguistic activity occurs in a variety of ways, and a characterization of language that is adequate to these many activities must be quite broad. Let me suggest such a characterization, making it more specific later, where it applies to cases of originative speaking.[1]

I take language to be a system of terms that constitutes a complex of meanings through the manipulation of a medium. There are as many languages as there are such systems. Speaking is one of the kinds of activities by which a language is operative, and sometimes, generated. Speaking is either an enactment of a pre-established language or it is a construction and advancement of a language. Thus, speaking is a kind of utterance brought about in the forming or structuring of materials.[2] When given structure through acts of speaking, the materials specify meanings.

---

[1] The adoption of this broad perspective on language is useful for examining the way metaphors that occur in verbal expressions are models of non-verbal as well as verbal creations. Thus I do not wish to insist that the term "language" must be taken in the most general sense. If someone were to object that it is misleading to extend the term beyond verbal contexts which serve the purposes of communications, then I would be willing to contract the scope of the term "language." But I would insist that the structure of verbal metaphors is common to the structure of creations in non-linguistic or non-verbal creations.

[2] The word "forming," of course, is not identical in meaning with the dubious word "Forming" which suggests that atemporal identities may be generated in time.

It should be emphasized that this description is intended to cover the generic characteristics of language and consequently all possible species of language, including non-verbal as well as verbal expressions. It is important to notice that I have not said that a system of terms must communicate meaning in order to be a language. It need only articulate meaning (though most linguistic articulations do communicate). If communication were essential, it would be questionable whether my characterization applies to the arts, or at least all examples of art. This description of language is intended to apply to gestures, the dance, painting, architecture, and music, as well as to spoken and written discourse. Moreover, verbal discourse may occur in trivial conversations, in scientific or philosophical reasoning, or in complex and abstract symbolization such as in logic and mathematics. Thus, in non-verbal articulation, a painting is a system of meanings and the act of painting is a kind of speaking. It consists in an articulation of meaning in a plastic medium, for it brings lines, colors, shapes, textures, etc., together so that they merge and take on visual meanings. Similiarly, gestures articulate meanings in the medium of determinate, controlled bodily movements. And a verbal expression is also an articulation in the medium of words and grammatical forms. It brings these together so that they determine verbal meanings.

In its breadth of application, this description of language does not delimit the problem of speech and novelty to any one form of language; but it does suggest that language is not found in all expressive activities. Not all bodily behavior is embodied speech. Some gestures are not lin-

By the term "forming," I mean the controlled activity of synthesizing elements in a medium. Thus, the stem, "form," in this context is not equated with Form in the sense of the atemporal determination exemplified in structure. I should point out also that in using the term "articulation" and "forming" my intention is to characterize language so that it includes either of two relationships between utterances and their meanings: on the one hand, an utterance may present meanings as immanent to the formed materials employed in the utterance; on the other hand, utterances may refer to meanings that transcend and are independent of the formed materials. I should also acknowledge that I assume that meanings are determinate objects of consciousness which may have a status independent of individual conscious acts. Even though meanings may be articulated in and through linguistic acts, such articulation may consist in discovering as well as generating meaning. Moreover, if a meaning is created, it can then endure in independence of the act that generated it, and consequently, it subsequently can be apprehended by an audience. This assumption is integral to the view that the requirements of created products are discovered as well as created and that there are evolutionary processes within which human actions take place. Meanings are possibilities for conscious attention, and they have a status in the world in which human consciousness exists. Meanings are constituted in what I have referred to as Forms and structures. They are the ingredients of intelligibility. Yet it is important to observe that the description of language as the articulation of meanings would hold whether or not one adopts the view that meanings are objective as well as resultant from articulating activities.

guistic. A grimace expressing pain, for instance, frequently is not, except in the case of an actor, a linguistic phenomenon. It is usually an involuntary, immediate response. It is not a forming of facial movements. Rather, it is a discharge of emotion, an ejection, an impulsive expression.[3] Similarly, to sneeze is to engage in an act that occurs through contortions of the face and sudden exhalation. Like a grimace, it is usually an involuntary reaction to the irritation that set it off, and it is not an act in which the sneezer forms bodily action in order to express meaning.

Meanings of course can be discovered in, or conferred upon, grimaces and sneezes. But to discover or confer meanings requires an interpretive act that is distinct from the grimace or the sneeze and that takes in a number of factors, such as remembered emotions and ideas, conditions in the environment, previous interpretations, etc., among which the grimace or the sneeze is only one factor. Indeed, in this context, the grimace or the sneeze is passive; it is given as part of the materials that are formed so that a meaning can be articulated by an interpreter. Only that activity is linguistic which is a modification of perceptual objects, including bodily behavior, in the service of consciousness directed toward giving form to what is modified.

The point that speech is the conscious articulation of meanings in a medium is important for clarifying the characteristics of creative speech. If an act of speech is originative, it must at least be a kind of forming. This is to say that a necessary condition of an instance of speaking which is originative is that it be founded on a conscious act of articulation, a selection of elements within a medium, and a merging of these so that the complex they constitute is coherent and meaningful.

To be sure, there is a sense in which every speech act may be identified as creative or originative. As an act of forming that occurs at a specific time and place, in a specific context, each speech act is individual and thus unique. It is a concrete expression and is unique in that it is qualified by temporal and spatial conditions and by subtle ways that distinguish it from every other speech act. This uniqueness, however, illustrates novelty of singularity, the kind of numerical novelty discussed earlier. Uniqueness of a linguistic expression does not of itself guarantee that the expression is creative in the sense that creative speech poses the problem in question: the origin of new intelligible meaning. The constructive function of most linguistic expressions is repetitive of meanings that already have been

---

[3] Both John Dewey, *op. cit.*, pp. 60 ff., and R. G. Collingwood, *op. cit., passim*, among others, hold views of art that depend upon this distinction between automatic response and conscious activity of expression.

articulated, no matter how unique the individual enactments. If speech acts were creative only be virtue of their special conditions and circumstances of enactment, then every occasion of speaking would be a "first" occasion and it would be unfamiliar. What would it mean, then, to say that someone had spoken before? It would mean that every time he had spoken, he had enacted speech for the first time. He could never repeat himself, and he could not call upon past resources provided by speech which could contribute to any present or future act of speech.

By contrast with familiar modes of speaking, creative speech yields meanings spoken for the first time, where "first" means being initially introduced into a language. Speech is creative when it is an articulation of what manifests not only the uniqueness that is present in every concrete articulation, but also a novelty in the meanings articulated. That is, newness must be present not only in the uniqueness of the *act* of speaking, but also in the intelligible character or *structure* of what is produced. Such origination may well be illustrated in the first man who spoke. But it is also illustrated when a word or meaning is first introduced into the system of words and meanings already present to man. Indeed, there is a sense in which creation within established language requires an even greater creative effort than the effort of the first man who spoke. For new meanings within a language must be created in spite of the weight of what is established and which is so much easier to recognize and repeat.

Creative speech, then, marks a break in an established system of meanings. The created meanings were not discernible in what was familiar before their introduction. They are thus unprecedented and surprising in the light of established language. In this sense, they appear to be created *ex nihilo*. This sense of *ex nihilo* creation is frequently overlooked. It is denied for the sake of maintaining continuity in the world and, ultimately, for the sake of one kind of hoped for intelligibility. But the fact that the determinist's intelligibility seems to be defied by the introduction into experience of the unfamiliar is not sufficient reason to reject the notion of creation *ex nihilo*. As suggested earlier, rejection of creation in this sense could be justified only if one could offer a proof that the world is fully intelligible and that metaphysical or ontological determinism is the only position which guarantees intelligibility.

I must emphasize that I do not intend to say that new meanings occur in a vacuum. I do not claim that new meanings have no antecedents in the elements of the medium and in articulations in that medium which precede the creation. However, as suggested by the description of Novelty Proper and the subsequent argument for affirming its reality, there are instances of the generation of meanings that were not predictable and which are not deducible from familiar meanings. The new meanings may be correlated with necessary antecedent conditions, but the correlations can be neither exhaustive nor identified without modifying our perspective on the antecedents. An attempt to trace what is new to its antecedents would require a revision of what had been familiar. In attempting to correlate an unfamiliar yet intelligible meaning and its past, established correlations are not available for identification. Neither the particular antecedents nor the particular connections which are relevant can be known until the new meaning is understood in its own terms. In order to determine what is relevant in the past, the function of the new meaning in the language into which it was introduced must be taken into account. The language as a whole is modified, and our understanding of the past that is relevant to the new meaning must be different subsequent to the advent of the new meaning.

If one traces the development of an artistic tradition, showing how old styles lead to new styles, one must do this in terms of the new styles, finding antecedents for what is new only after the new is given and is suggestive of what can be imposed on the previous styles. Baroque art, for example, can be viewed as an outgrowth of renaissance art, but what seems significant in renaissance art as a preparation for the Baroque depends upon the perspective made possible because of the origin of Baroque art. Giotto's way of freeing figures in space may be seen as a precedent for Michelangelo's way of exhibiting the powerful movement of massive shapes. But the identification of Giotto's way of freeing figures, and his breaking with the stabilized figures in the conventions that preceded him, is made possible by what is discovered in Michelangelo.

In the context of verbal language, it can be argued that a word such as "spirit," which is now taken in a non-physical sense and ordinarily traced to "breath" or "wind," may well have functioned in the past as a non-physical basis for the very terms to which it is now ordinarily traced.[4] In other words, a term such as "breath" or "wind," to which "spirit" is now traced must, at a time in the past, have had a fundamental meaning that was equally non-physical and physical; otherwise, the transition from "breath" or "spirit" that led to the current meaning of "spirit" would have been sheer accident. In any case, "spirit" taken in its own contemporary significance does affect past meanings. It throws light on "breath," just as much as "breath" is understood to be a term from which "spirit" is

[4] See Owen Barfield, "The Meaning of the World 'Literal,'" in *Metaphor and Symbol* (London: Butterworths Scientific Publication, 1960), pp. 48-63.

derived. This can be seen in the way current understanding of the term "spirit," in poetry such as Keats's, has affected aspects or overtones of the meaning of the term "wind" – giving this "physical" term some kinship with self-conscious awareness of what is felt to be internal to human beings.

2. Speech and Implements

In order to help sharpen the point that new meanings cannot be given initially by direct, discursive speech, I should like to compare briefly the function of language with the use of implements. I wish to suggest that the media of speech can be viewed as sets of implements. The pigments used in painting, the sounds used in composing music, the words used in constructing verbal expressions, etc., may be thought of as implements, because they are things manipulated for certain purposes, articulating meaning. They are means to an end.

What are the purposes distinctive of linguistic implements used in originative speech? Toward what meanings is creative speech aimed? The ready answer to this question is that creative speech is intended to express new meanings. Its implements are used for new purposes. But this obvious answer points once again to the fundamental puzzle encountered in understanding creativity. The requirement that an ordinary implement or tool, such as a hammer or a pair of spectacles, be used for a new purpose presents two difficulties. First, the tool must be used in a way for which it is not already fitted. Of course, such a use might be carried out. But, in that case, the tool involved would need to be understood differently in order to serve its new purpose; and if it were to serve that purpose most effectively, it would need to be modified. As suggested in the first chapter, the primary utility would need to be shifted. Thus, specific elements of a medium of speech which is originative would need to be used differently, and the elements introduced into the product would need to be changed with respect to their established characteristics in order to serve purposes for which that medium is not already fitted. In verbal speech, new terms – words, or complexes of words in phrases and sentences – may be needed and new ways of expression must be affected in order to serve the new purposes. The act of origination would necessarily modify language and create new meanings at one stroke.

The intimacy of implement and end, or of medium and articulated meaning, in originative speech suggests that speech must become artistic as it becomes creative. That is, it must treat its implements in neutral terms and for their own sakes, independently of the purposes to which they are usually put, in order to transform their functions. The medium must be regarded not as transparent, as pointing beyond itself, to an antecedent use, but as transformed in some way. I shall return later to this point about the role of art in originative speech.

There is a second, perhaps more difficult problem raised by the requirement that an implement serve a purpose other than that for which the implement was originally constructed. Shift in purpose in the case of originative speech is not simply a transference from one established purpose to another known purpose. The purposes of originative speech are not given before such speech has been changed so that it achieves the different purpose. The meanings to be articulated are at best vaguely defined for the speaker. As an originator, the speaker does not know until he has originated the new meanings just what those meanings are. He does not have a ready-made target at which to aim. He must discover the new meanings as he refashions the language with which he creatively articulates them. On the one hand, the medium he uses must cease to serve as a set of implements designed for familiar articulations of meanings. On the other hand, the medium – the materials of the painter, the tones of the composer, the gestures known to the choreographer, or the words available for the verbal speaker – cannot be handled by the creators in any one of these media as implements intended for a preconceived new meaning. Paradoxically, they must be used with knowledge only of their familiar purposes so that they deny these purposes for the sake of accomplishing purposes for which they are not yet designed. They must be used directly to express familiar meanings which at the same time deny these familiar meanings in the service of not-yet-determined, new meanings.

The materials of speech, then, must be regarded by the originator in two ways. They must be seen as having conventionally familiar meanings and also as not having these meanings. They must be seen as implements with defined purposes and as objects in their own right, ready to be something more than they already are in their familiar aspect. While it is being formed, originative speech means familiarly in a direct way and means newly in an indirect, oblique way.

A central problem which faces us, then, is to explore further the way speech takes on this double function, articulating conventionally familiar meanings while indirectly forming new meanings. This two-fold function can be described with reference to a feature of the evolution of language that is ordinarily minimized, if not ignored. This feature is a necessary condition of creative speech. Creative speech must employ familiar words

LANGUAGE AND AESTHETIC STRUCTURE OF NOVELTY

in ways that are in tension, in ways that are initially incoherent in the context of established language. The incoherence which is introduced is the condition for the initially secondary, indirect function of the speech as it forms new meaning.

To say that speech can mean obliquely through a tension within what is articulated in familiar meanings is to say that the speaker must hint at what he says. He must do this because he cannot say directly what is new. He has neither meanings nor means at his disposal to do so. At the outset of his speaking, he has available only forms of expression with which he is familiar. Consequently, he forces familiar words and manners of expressions into peculiar, tension-ridden formulations, thereby requiring himself as well as us to attend to something more than the familiar meanings. The incoherence and incompleteness of the familiar meanings in originative speech is evidenced in the problems – and, I think, the impossibility – of finding a complete translation in conventional terms of expressions that are original.

The forming of expressions so that they exhibit incoherence or tension and thereby present indirect meaning is illustrated in metaphorical expression. Taking metaphor as model, we can see how words are manipulated so that they mean obliquely through an inner tension of familiar meanings.

B. SPEECH AND METAPHORS

1. Indirect Speech and Metaphor in Art, Science, and Philosophy

Before examining directly metaphorical expression, it is necessary to make a few preliminary remarks. First of all, in discussing metaphorical expressions, I shall consider metaphors as they appear in poetic language. Metaphorical expression, of course, is not restricted to poetry. The suggestion that speech which is creative must be obilque is applicable to all species of language. I have already indicated ways in which metaphors invade discursive language, particularly in philosophical discussions. Scientific discourse as well as poetry and the various arts must, I think, be oblique in order to be originative.[5] Illustration of this broad application of the

---

[5] I refer to scientific discourse that is interpretive of the world. Whether creation in uninterpreted mathematics is metaphorical is a difficult issue, and I suspect that if applied in such a field, the notion of metaphor would need to be modified drastically. Unfortunately, I cannot explore the relation of metaphor to creativity in the development of scientific hypotheses. If metaphorical thinking is part of the construction of scientific hypotheses, then creativity in science and art must be fundamentally alike. On the other hand, if metaphorical thinking is not part of creation in science, then

suggestion would be a difficult and extensive project, and it might well be that the proposal would need to be qualified in a number of ways when applied to creative speech in science. But surely, as already suggested, originative philosophical language includes analogical arguments, poetic language, artistic devices, and expressions intended to evoke insights that cannot be delineated in precise statements. Plato resorted to analogies, Socratic irony, the form of the dialogue, and myth. Sartre incorporated metaphor in his arguments. Moreover, philosophers less deliberately artistic in expression, such as Aristotle and Spinoza, brought words together in ways different from their predecessors so as to propel the reader's understanding toward insights that could be gained only by transcending the series of statements presented in the form of discursive argument.

Of course, speech that is not originative, but which conveys or articulates what is established in its language, may also have indirect meanings associated with it. But these indirect meanings are, for the primary purposes of conventional speech, overlooked. Moreover, there is no guarantee that what is thus indirectly meant is new or that it is anything more than additional associations or connections. In fact, on the view I propose, the indirect meanings of conventional speech are not antecedent associations waiting to be noticed. They are new meanings made possible because they are connected with the familiar meanings that are metaphorically construed by a creator who gives established meanings an unconventional "turn." However, once a new meaning is brought into focus, we may, depending on our purposes, overlook the originative and oblique character which such speech once had. Metaphors assimilated into a language lose their freshness; they become familiar and function literally and no longer originatively. It is only in language that retains its aesthetic character, only in metaphors that continue to be regarded as metaphorical, that we are reminded of the creative function of speech.

It is true that we sometimes seem to succeed in extracting certain new meanings from aesthetic creations and in fixing these meanings so that they are reduced to what is familiar. But at the same time, live metaphors

---

science must be interpreted as essentially a kind of problem solving where all the criteria of a solution are antecedently known. It is significant that Donald Schon, in *The Displacement of Concepts* (London: Tavistock Publications, 1964), has interpreted scientific creativity as essentially metaphorical. Colin Turbayne's interpretation of metaphor in *The Myth of Metaphor* (New Haven, Connecticut: Yale University Press, 1962), while excluding the possibility of radical newness, does support the view that scientific theory uses metaphors as models. Although I cannot agree with all that Schon or Turbayne say about metaphor, I shall dogmatically appeal to what seems to be the plausible position that metaphorical thinking is integral to the origin of new ideas in science as well as art. In any case, even if my analysis of novelty does not apply to science, I nevertheless contend that the analysis does apply in art.

and successful art sustain their originative characters, exhibiting through indirection a rich, perhaps inexhaustible range of new meanings. This, of course, is why it is so easy to turn to art and metaphor to illustrate the characteristics of creative speech.

As I have indicated, in concentrating on metaphors I also give art a primary role in characterizing the structure of creativity. Works of art as well as metaphorical expressions are taken to be models of creations, though metaphors show more economically the features to be singled out. It is important to keep in mind that the chief reason art is taken as a key is that works of art have served as prime instances of creativity for artists, art critics, and inquirers in general. I am simply choosing the kind of thing that already has been identified as a created product.

As examples of creations, works of art are a basis for the acknowledgement of creativity. Perhaps, without them, creativity would not have been seen as a problem. Yet the description of Novelty Proper can be entertained without reference to art, and it can be compared with descriptions of what is regarded as new in products outside the realm of art. Still, the description of structures that present themselves as different for the first time shares common ground with a description of the structure of works of art generally, or what in the context of aesthetic theory is often called the aesthetic object. Whether the claim that every work of art must conform to such a description – exhibiting something like an organic unity or an order whose parts are internally related – may be disputed. I shall consider this problem later. However, the minimal claim which is crucial here is restricted to the necessary conditions for objects to be recognized as new in the sense in which certain phenomena, namely, the products of creative activities, have provoked special interest in creativity. These conditions for which I have argued earlier are found in at least some works of art, if they are found anywhere. It is for this reason that I rely on consideration of the structure of works of art, and, for the moment, metaphors, in order to develop the model for the aesthetic understanding of created objects and, in turn, a model for understanding creative acts.

Metaphorical expression is singularly appropriate to discriminating the structure of works of art. In saying this, I assume that metaphorical expressions play a dominant role in the clearest examples of art in the verbal medium. Even if one rejects the suggestion that poems are extended metaphors, one can hardly deny that poems do include metaphors and that metaphors are crucial in constituting the created character or new meanings immanent within those poems. In any case, individual instances of metaphors are at least sometimes instances of linguistic expressions that contribute new meaning to a language. In terms of the vocabulary I have used, they are the simplest instances of Novelty Proper. Thus, their structure should be clearly evident and most readily available for close examination.

2. Metaphors and the Organic Character of Art

At this point, let me acknowledge an assumption which lies behind what I have been saying about metaphors and created objects. What has been said about the interrelation of components in a metaphor is the kernel of an aesthetics which asserts that works of art are autonomous and that they exhibit meanings immanent to them.[6] This internality of meaning can be seen in metaphors, and I shall here treat metaphors as miniature examples of works of art, at least with respect to the functioning of their constituents and the presentation of new meanings. As in each work of art, the elements which are discriminable within it are held together in a structure that is initially unduplicated elsewhere.

The work of art, then, appears to be created in exhibiting its own meaning in its own structure; it is autonomous as a determinate structure which exemplifies a Form initially discoverable nowhere but through its own structure. Its character is not describable in terms of features it shares with other members of its species or with any other particulars said to share

[6] The view assumed here may be challenged. There are various positions taken in aesthetics, and, in particular, in recent art criticism, that oppose the theory of art which I assume. In this context, I shall attempt no more than to assert rather dogmatically the theory, and appeal to the fact that it is widely known and has been discussed and developed sufficiently for me to refer the reader to other writings for a defense of the view I shall assume. In particular, I believe that arguments for the autonomy of art in B. Croce (*Aesthetic as Science of Expression and General Linguistics* [New York: Macmillan and Co., 1922]), R. G. Collingwood, (*op. cit.*), Eliseo Vivas (*Creation and Discovery, Essays in Criticism and Aesthetics, op. cit., passim*), Morris Weitz (in his earlier aesthetic theory, in *Philosophy of the Arts* [Cambridge, Massachusetts: Harvard University Press, 1950]) are still convincing, in spite of the fact that Weitz has modified his view in his more recent writings. It also may be observed that even if the theory were not acceptable, its value in this study depends not upon its adequacy as a theory of art in general, but on its adequacy in describing objects that exhibit Novelty Proper. Thus, if one does not agree with the description as a theory of art in general, let the description be taken as appropriate only to one aspect of art and not as a theory providing a definition of art or a claim that autonomy in an object guarantees it to be a work of art. Even if one were, for instance, to adopt the claim that the concept of art is open-textured, what I assume about the autonomy of the meaning of art with respect to its novelty would not be undermined. I shall offer later a comparison of my interpretation of Form and metaphor with the notion of "family resemblance." My comparison should show that the concept "art" may be open-textured. However, the openness of the term "art" is not the same as openness of an individual artistic creation to an indeterminate range of requirements to be met by the strands of meaning relevant to new meanings in individual works.

with it common qualities. With respect to the qualities that participate in its structure, it is self-determined. Thus, the object in which Novelty Proper occurs discloses meaning which is self-determined in the sense that the object maintains its distinct nature by gathering in its qualities and holding them in a whole that approaches an identity that is unique. And since this identity around which the qualities of the object cluster is different from any other identity that went before it, it is a negation of the world – a negation of all identities preceding and contemporaneous with it. But since it is also determinate, since it requires its components, it is an affirmation as well as a negation. It is this positive autonomy that is often connoted by such terms of approbation as "freshness," "originality," "creative," and, sometimes "individuality."

Perhaps it is easiest to amplify this account of the autonomy of art by making an appeal to the concept of organic unity. Although this concept is drawn from biology, it is often used as an analogy in aesthetic theory. An object whose unity is organic is constituted so that addition or elimination of any element changes the character of the whole. Thus, all aspects of the whole are interwoven so that they are mutually interdependent. All the elements that compose it – its formal traits, expressed ideas, suggestions of mood, etc. – affect one another. The whole determines the characters of the parts, and the parts determine the identity of the whole. To cite an example from poetry, if one were to replace the word "quietness" with "stillness" or "silence" in Keats's expression "still unravished bride of quietness," from his "Ode on a Grecian Urn," the line in which the expression occurs, the stanza, and indeed, the entire poem, would be changed. The word "silence" (or "stillness") would present a different sound and different rhythm within the pattern established by Keats's poem, and this different sound would affect the total sound value by introducing a different tone and a certain abruptness in the rhythm. But more important, the substituted words suggest connotative meanings different from those which Keats put there. "Stillness," for instance, is more likely to suggest immobility than is quietness. "Silence," on the other hand, lacks the connotation of physical endurance.

One of the objections to the thesis that a work of art is like an organic unity is that elements in art are not all equally important and that some elements can be eliminated without changing the central character of the work as art. I do not believe this objection contradicts the notion of organic unity. There are, at least in some works of art, certain changes that may be brought about by addition or elimination of elements and that do not radically alter those works as wholes. This depends upon where the change occurs in relation to a hierarchy of elements. Some elements are more central or dominant than others; in such situations, changes in less dominant elements are not so noticeable, since they function less pervasively. For example, the absence of a leaf on a tree in a Cézanne landscape would be less significant to the whole painting than would the absence of a mountain peak or a change in the direction of an entire tree. Hierarchical organization is also present in a biological organic unity, and it should not be a surprising notion – though it is often overlooked by critics of the theory that art is organic. The absence of a finger, for instance, yields a difference to the whole organism. But it is not as effective in changing the character of the whole as is the absence of an arm.

In any case, the structure of a work of art is immanent. Whatever can be discriminated as a part of the whole cannot be conceptualized and extracted from the whole without some loss of meaning, both for the part when it functions as a component of the whole and for the whole with all of its parts functioning together. Thus, the meanings present in the work of art are dependent upon this internal identity. At the same time, the internal structure of the work is not a Form that can be thought about independently of the work. The Form depends upon what in the first chapter was called structure, that is, the concrete complex of components that comprise the product.

In order to view this concept of the internal structure of art from another perspective, it will be helpful to turn again to several observations about what is generally thought to happen during the stages of the creative process.[7] Stages in which preparatory groping, and, as frequently claimed, incubation or non-conscious or unconscious mental activity occur are followed by the crucial stage often called "illumination" or "insight." This stage, in turn, is followed by an elaboration or perfecting of what was achieved in illumination. It is during the crucial stage of illumination that the radical break with the past either occurs or is made possible. It is this stage which is ordinarily recognized as the moment of the creative leap when the creator most intensely realizes or begins to recognize the novel structure which he has been struggling to define. Now, even if we doubt the adequacy of a description that distinguishes the creative process into discrete stages, we can observe an essential feature of the moment or aspect of the creative act which yields what is new. As already emphasized, the initial insight into the way of synthesizing data so as to constitute the

---

[7] What has become the classical statement of distinct stages now assumed in much psychological literature is credited to Graham Wallas, *The Art of Thought* (New York: Harcourt, Brace and Company, 1926), pp. 79-107.

internal structure was not envisaged before the artist began the creative process. If he did not foresee a Form to which to conform, if the Form is discovered as he creates, then the Form must be discerned through a structure that is immanent to the totality of elements that comprise the created object.

With this acknowledgement of the concept of art and its paradoxical consequences in mind, I shall turn to a consideration of metaphorical expression. Even if metaphors may occur outside an explicit aesthetic context, they are, as I have already proposed, integral to the structures of works of verbal art and to the created characters of these works.

3. *Metaphors as Constitutive Negations*

When Aristotle said, "Metaphor consists in giving the thing a name that belongs to something else. . . ." he indicated a crucial feature of metaphorical expression, no matter by what interpretation one develops Aristotle's succinct statement.[8] An expression that functions metaphorically alters reference, and for Aristotle and a number of other writers this alternation is a kind of transferrence. The conventional reference of a familiar word is transferred to an unconventional reference. "Rosy-fingered dawn" gives a time of day a name that conventionally belongs to something else by transferring the reference of "rosy-fingered." To speak of "the warmth of his personality" is to give to personality the term "warmth," which does not "literally" belong to personality, since "warmth" refers "literally" or conventionally to a moderate degree of physically and perceptually felt heat.[9] Or, to cite again "Ode on a Grecian

---

[8] Aristotle, *Poetics,* translated by Ingram Bywater, 1457b. Views of metaphorical expression which are most directly related to the approach suggested here are found in: Monroe C. Beardsley, *Aesthetics: Problems in the Philosophy of Criticism* (New York: Harcourt, Brace, 1958), and "The Metaphorical Twist," *Philosophy and Phenomenological Research* XXII, No. 3 (March, 1962), 293-307; Mikel Dufrenne, *Language and Philosophy* (Bloomington: Indiana University Press, 1963); James Edie, "Expression and Metaphor," *Philosophy and Phenomenological Research* XXIII, No. 4 (June, 1963), 538-561; Paul Henle, in *Language, Thought and Culture,* edited by Paul Henle (Ann Arbor, Michigan: The University of Michigan Press, 1965), Chapter 7; and Philip Wheelwright, *Metaphor and Reality* (Bloomington, Indiana: Indiana University Press, 1962). These views have been helpful to me. However, my own interpretation of metaphor first occurred to me independently of theirs.

[9] The term "literal" is used here to refer to what is both conventional and intelligible with reference to physical reality, or experience understood by ordinary thinking, as well as science, to be verifiable. Problems in using the term "literal" have been interestingly discussed by Owen Barfield, *op. cit.* Let me point out too that here and throughout the discussion of metaphor, I shall speak in terms of the object, that is, the metaphorical expression and its structure, as well as from the perspective of hearers and readers who respond to metaphors. I shall take the features of the object

Urn," Keats refers to an urn as "thou still unravished bride of quietness," thus using terms that literally or conventionally apply to other things: An urn is not a person about to be married; nor is an inanimate object such as an urn the kind of thing which is literally quiet.

These examples and Aristotle's definition make clear that when metaphors are used, meanings understood in one context shift to meanings offered for understanding in another context. The standard account of such shifts, which is also offered by Aristotle, is that they are comparisons. The thing to which the strange term or expression is applied is compared with at least some of the meanings of the strange term. In "rosy-fingered dawn," the sky at dawn is compared with the spreading elongated shape of fingers. In "the warmth of his personality," a personality is compared with the moderately intensified quality of heat. The comparisons that metaphors express are generally thought to be based upon "similarities of dissimilars," to use Aristotle's expression.[10] On this view, a metaphor combines concepts or meanings and calls attention to formerly unrecognized comparisons based upon similarities. Metaphors are stated comparisons or implied comparisons in which the two things compared are identified. The comparison of course, is implicit. Unlike similes, metaphors withhold explicit statement that a comparison is being made.

I shall not attempt to summarize the varieties of comparison theories that can be found in the literature on metaphor. However, I do want to mention several reasons for not accepting this traditional interpretation. I am not alone in rejecting the tradition. A number of writers have argued against it and have developed views of their own. I shall rely on some of these views only where they are especially suggestive for my consideration of speech acts that exhibit radical novelty.

In the first place, it should be obvious that metaphorical expressions do not make ordinary comparisons. The similarities said to be found in dissimilars cannot be familiar and readily evident for those who look. Aristotle himself regarded the metaphorical act as extraordinary. Thus, he says that it is something "that cannot be learned from others" and is a sign of genius requiring "intuitive perception."[11] Further, observation (granted by proponents of this interpretation) that the comparison is not explicit should itself be sufficient to raise suspicion. That the comparison is not explicit is a clue that the traditional view is interpretive as well as

to serve as conditions for, and to be correlative with, characteristics of the response. If a distinction between object and observer is significant, I shall make this explicit.
[10] *Op. cit.*, 1459a.
[11] *Ibid.*

descriptive and that the metaphorical comparison is an unusual kind of comparison. Even more striking is the condition that similarities suggested by metaphors must be found in dissimilars. A metaphor is supposed to perform a function while hiding the fact that it does so, and it is supposed to show something through what that thing is not. These peculiarities surely are grounds for questioning all straightforward and unqualified versions of the standard comparison theory.

The comparison view implies the possibility of translating or paraphrasing a metaphor into familiar and antecedently understood meanings. It implies that we can state the comparison, identify a similarity not seen before, and thereby say in conventional terms what the metaphor means. The possibility of a perfect translation of metaphors which generate new meanings, however, must be rejected, for reasons like those already offered for denying a reductionism of radical newness to the past. An attempt to translate the expression "winged words" into "rapid communication," for example, misses a crucial component of the meaning; otherwise, "rapid communication" or perhaps some other simple translation would serve as well as the metaphor.[12] To be sure, if a metaphor is "dead" (or no longer responded to as presenting a new meaning), then another translation may do, as in cases where it is possible to substitute a synonymous expression.

---

[12] I should point out that my objections to paraphrase do not depend upon what Beardsley objects to in the "Object Comparison Theory," "The Metaphorical Twist," *op. cit.* Beardsley objects to the intervention of an object of one of the terms (the "tenor") in a metaphor which is compared with the subject (the "vehicle") of the metaphor. Thus, on the view he claims to oppose, the transferred name (that does not belong to the object of the subject) is supposed to have an object with properties that are explicitly meant in the metaphor ("The Metaphorical Twist," *op. cit.*, pp. 295-296). While I agree with Beardsley's objections to interpreting metaphors through reference to such supposed objects, I think the point of his criticism can be made whether or not any specific object is mentioned. The point concerns the difficulties in attempts to explain metaphors by translating them into correlations of properties drawn from different contexts. What deserves criticism, then, is the dubiousness of any identification of correlated properties of objects that are metaphorically transferred to the object of the subject. What is crucial, I think, is that any specification of properties identified in terms of conventional contexts misses the mark of the meaning of the metaphor. Beardsley's account of metaphorical meaning as based on a "twist" from central to marginal meaning also seems to skirt the main point – in spite of his claims that his view affirms novelty – that is, whether all appeals to formerly identifiable meanings are sufficient to account for the newness of meaning generated in the metaphor. Beardsley's theory requires the interpreter to find non-standardized secondary or peripheral properties already there but *rearranged* for cognition in the act of understanding the metaphor (*ibid.*, pp. 301-305). What is new for him is the "new status" of relevant or "eligible" properties. I see no essential difference between his theory and the view that metaphors are implied comparisons based on formerly neglected similarities or antecedent meanings construed to have continuity with the subject of the metaphor. What Beardsley fails to take into account is the way in which the "new status" is itself constitutive of an additional meaning not identical with the sum of the meanings of the secondary or peripheral properties.

Moreover, for some purposes, a partial translation of a "live" new metaphor might do, if all that is needed is transmission of information, say, about someone's ability to communicate.

In any case, in the context of the problems of paraphrasing metaphors, we should notice that if the comparison theory were true, language could not grow qualitatively. My point here, of course, depends upon assuming that if such a theory applies to metaphor, then it is intended to apply to all instances of speech. If this were not so, it is difficult to see why untranslatability of linguistic units should be denied of metaphor, where change in language seems most obvious. If a paraphrase were available for every new expression, then language would be ready-made. All its resources would be given and – not to speak of the question of how language could have originated in the first place – all meanings preformed and prepared to substitute for all purported additions.

Language could expand quantitatively by the introduction of invented and stipulated terms (technical jargon), neologisms for what is established, and different combinations of words with different relations of meanings. But such growth would consist in greater numbers of words and combinations of words and meanings already there and already familiar. There could be no growth of a language in the sense that new meanings are introduced. Let me emphasize here (and this is a point I made in a different context) that it will not do to say that the recombinations and adjusted relations are what is new, unless one grants that these combinations and relations are construed as syntheses or at least as combinations with different, formerly unrecognized meanings providing added resources for speaking. In that case, the growth of language qualitatively is affirmed, but the possibility of a fully adequate translation must be either abandoned, or accepted only as an unfamiliar and new expression substituted for the expression to be translated. The translation, then, would need translating, and so on, *ad infinitum*.[13]

---

[13] This point can be made in terms of what are said to be "similarities of dissimilarities." Suppose that language changes through the rearranging of terms so that they refer to formerly unrecognized similarities. Either these similarities are themselves unprecedented, or they were antecedently present, waiting to be referred to. On the first alternative, the translation or different combination of terms in the language that refers to "new" similarities would need to include unprecedented combinations that are not exhausted by antecedent references. The combination offered in the translation would itself contribute to the qualitative growth of language. It would need to articulate what was unfamiliar in an unfamiliar way. On the second alternative, the changed language would include combinations that refer to what was antecedent but unnoticed and unfamiliar, and the combinations too would need to do so in unfamiliar ways, as does a metaphor; otherwise they would not refer to the unfamiliar antecedent similarities. But then what is at issue concerns the way or manner of combination. If the manner of combining familiar terms is unfamiliar, then

I do not wish to repudiate the comparison theory in its entirety. I think it is partially correct. Metaphors do transfer terms and their meanings from conventionally accepted contexts to unconventional contexts. And they do present comparisons. Such comparisons enter into metaphors and they do so in varying degrees of relevance to the metaphorical meanings. But at least in some metaphors the comparisons are not sufficient to provide the basis of an exhaustive translation. Even so direct a comparison as "rosy-fingered dawn" presents a formerly unconventional perspective on a time of day, integrating meanings taken from differing contexts so that qualities of redness, fingers, and dawn converge in a unit. All three terms appear differently when brought together than they do when taken separately.[14] And reformulation of the metaphor in discursive language can do no more than cite common qualities recognizable apart from the meanings of the three terms.

It was said above that even the traditional interpretation of metaphor acknowledges pecularities about the way metaphorical expressions offer comparisons. The comparisons are not offered explicitly as comparisons, and they are constituted in dissimilars. The extraordinary character of metaphorical expressions is a clue to the special structure of metaphors. The key to this peculiarity is evident in the prefix "dis-" that alerts us to the negation in that which generates metaphorical meaning. However true it may be that metaphors draw comparisons, and however varied the theories about the way such comparisons can be interpreted, this negative aspect is not given sufficient emphasis, even though it is acknowledged. The presence of negation is essential to the manifestation of metaphorical function and the ensuing new meaning.

The negative quality of metaphors is indicated not only in Aristotle's use of the term "dissimilars" but also in his general description of metaphor. The connection of one term with another in newly formed metaphors relates two items *not* conventionally brought together in language. One term or, more generally, one concept, is related to something to which the concept conventionally is *not* appropriate. The expression "winged words" is a metaphor that negates by presenting something for thought which did not exist from the standpoint of the conventional meanings of

the combination is an integration of terms and a synthesis in which a different, unfamiliar meaning contributes to language. Thus, if such a combination could be translated, the translation would need to offer an unfamiliar way of meaning what the metaphor means.

[14] Paul Henle, in *Language, Thought and Culture, op. cit.*, Chapter 7, refers to the basis of reference of metaphor that is not simply provided by antecedent similarities as "induced similarity." Philip Wheelwright refers to this aspect of metaphor as its "diaphoric" movement: *Metaphor and Reality, op. cit.*, especially Chapter Four.

each of the words considered apart from their conjunction. From the perspective of literal thought the expression is conceptually incoherent, and it refers to what is not actually present in the world as a physical object. Words do not actually have wings. The metaphor calls attention to certain meanings or connotations of the word "wing" (such as swiftness and flight) in conjunction with connotations of "words" (such as "communication" and "verbal expression"). Yet the expression does not literally refer to verbal utterances with attached organs, but it does mean something like (though not exactly like) rapid communication.

Hence, a metaphor that functions so as to say something other than what can be said by another conventional or literal expression does have a partial basis in what is already known, but this partial basis does not consist in simply revealing an affinity; it does not merely call attention to unnoticed similarities. Indeed, such similarities are less relevant than dissimilarities, for the tension between two disparate terms is required for the expression to function, and the contrast and opposition between the terms gives form to the interaction between them such that they yield an integration. The contrast of their normal roles in conventional and formerly established contexts affects this interaction and makes possible a different context in which the terms of the metaphor exhibit integrated opposition. "Winged words" shows on the one hand what words as ordinarily understood are not and, on the other hand, what being winged as ordinarily understood is not. "Rosy-fingered dawn" shows what a certain time of day, conventionally understood, is not and what literally being rosy-fingered is not. These exhibited contrasts are at least as important to each expression, taken as a whole, as are any affinities that are indicated. And it is these contrasts that give form to the integration of meanings in the unprecedented metaphorical context.

A metaphor, then, calls attention to what, for established concepts, is not the case; and in doing so, it emphasizes a tension between determinate and familiar concepts. From the standpoint of the thinker or experiencing subject, it disrupts his conceptualization of the world. From the standpoint of the world already known, it discloses disruptions in continuities. It reveals a break in established patterns. It negates the past viewed as the *status quo*. And in offering an unprecedented meaning through disclosing a gap in a rational pattern, a metaphorical expression manifests itself to us as an instance of novelty.

If a metaphor is preferable to more literal or conventional language, then the metaphor must present its own meaning – a meaning not fully given in any other current expression. Thus, if "winged words" is still "fresh" as a metaphor, the word "winged" does not simply mean swiftness or flight. It may suggest this, but it means more – what makes flight possible, something that is light, something that soars. Its meaning takes on a special character when it is brought into focus with the other term, "words." Thus "words," in this context, does not mean, simply, verbal utterances or communication. Its meanings, too, interpenetrate with the meanings of "winged." The term "winged" interacts with "words" to suggest verbal expressions that are airy and rising and that consequently are both swifter and more noble than mere words. The resultant metaphorical meaning is unique.

I wish to emphasize that the unique and new meaning presented by metaphorical expression is discerned through and is based upon the negative aspect of the metaphor. The presence of a meaning that is not exhausted by the combination of terms when they are interpreted in their literal meanings is implied by the incompatibility of those meanings. This point is made from the standpoint of the object: the metaphor and its components. It also must be made from the standpoint of the knower. If the metaphor is unfamiliar, not having passed into the language so that its unique meaning is taken for granted, then the incoherence of the expression invokes the hearer or reader to shift attention, to regard the articulation as transcending the literally construed connotations, and to apprehend a meaning not given in a literal translation, such as "swift communication." [15] The reader or hearer is invited to discover qualities that are focused in an untranslatable unity of meanings. This interpretative activity need not take place in a series of temporally related steps, unless intellectual puzzlement about the metaphor is so great that the reader or hearer becomes self-conscious about apprehending the meaning of the expression. More likely is a reading or hearing that grasps the meaning quickly in a Gestalt that is seen in some larger context in which the metaphor appears.

Let me now develop the point that metaphors depend upon negations by considering again the peculiarities of metaphors, but now with special emphasis on several examples from poetry. With these examples in mind, I shall examine more closely the negation that I have ascribed to metaphor. It is obvious that the easiest way to single out metaphors is to look for them in poetic speech. Indeed, there is reason to consider an entire poem as an extended metaphor. This is to be expected, for poetic speech is a species of verbal language in which the speaker plays with meaning.

---

[15] The role of contrast as a condition for the appropriate response of the observer has been emphasized and discussed by both Henle and Beardsley.

However, if it is correct to say that a poem not only includes metaphors but also, as a whole, is itself a metaphor, a difficulty arises. When we try to extract a metaphorical expression from poetry in order to consider how it may exhibit a new meaning, we risk distorting the extracted expression. Characterization of the expression, when it is taken out of context which is itself metaphorical, must be incomplete, for, as a constituent of the poem, the function of the expression depends upon the whole to which it belongs.

Because of this difficulty, it is advisable to begin by selecting for illustration a phrase from a well known part of a famous literary work. In such a case, some sense of the whole can be presupposed. The phrase I select is "when we have shuffled off this mortal coil," taken from Shakespeare's *Hamlet*. It is clear that the expression joins words so that they bring into focus meanings different from the meanings associated with their familiar usages – i.e., from the senses which they must have had in their familiar contexts before Shakespeare used them in his play. The words must function as indirectly meaningful by coming together as a convergence of meanings, each of which in itself misses the meaning exhibited by the whole phrase, but all of which work together to generate that meaning. For instance, the phrase might be translated somewhat directly as "when we have died." But in the context of Hamlet's soliloquy this translation surely misses the mark. It leads away from the core of meaning suggested by the phrase and required by the larger context. The phrase might also be translated, somewhat less directly, as "when we have thrown off this bodily shell," or, "when we have extricated ourselves from this mortal turmoil." But these paraphrases are also inadequate, for they are not adequate to the concentration of meanings presented. They fall short of the richness of meaning articulated by Shakespeare, a richness that includes the unity of the meanings of dying, releasing the soul from the body, being free of trouble contained in bodily existence, and the relation of these to fears of a troubled soul that hesitates not simply about death but also about worldly responsibility.

Another example of a metaphorical expression may be extracted from Wallace Stevens' poem, "The Man With the Blue Guitar." [16] In this example, I shall not presuppose the entire poetic context, since I believe the metaphor can be treated for its most crucial meaning even though it is taken out of this context. In any case, it is illustrative and useful for a closer analysis of the interactions of the meanings of the kinds of metaphors that are creations.

---

[16] *Opus Posthumous* (New York: Knopf, 1957), p. 73.

Let us consider two lines from this poem:

> "The greenish quaverings of day
> Quiver upon the blue guitar."

We should observe that this metaphorical expression is complex, including metaphor within metaphor. The expression "greenish quaverings of day" is itself a metaphor that merges metaphorically with the expression, "quiver upon the blue guitar." It will be helpful to isolate and concentrate on the first metaphor. This can be done, I think, without violating the larger metaphorical context.

I should like to consider the expression "The greenish quaverings of day" with respect to its parts. As a general thesis about the parts of a metaphor, I shall make several distinctions. The parts of a metaphor can be regarded in one or more of three ways: as constituents, as antecedent elements, and as subsequent or consequent elements.

Antecedent elements are the terms extracted from the metaphor and interpreted in their formerly accepted meanings. Constituents are the terms regarded as components in their internal interaction. Consequent elements are the terms extracted again (as in some analyses of works of art) and viewed as transformed elements, having meanings that are made possible by the interaction of terms when they function as constituents.

It should be pointed out that the transformation of elements is not simply the result of shifting attention from conventionally acknowledged properties connoted by the antecedent elements to properties not heretofore associated with them. It is not simply a matter of highlighting accidental properties potentially associated with the terms in their function as antecedent elements. Such shifting of attention and highlighting does take place, and the shift occurs when there is recognition of the way the terms, functioning as antecedent elements, are relevant to the terms functioning as constituents and as consequent elements. But the transformation of terms into constituents and their function as consequent elements makes possible the shift of attention. Without the new added meaning issuing from the terms in their constitutive function, there would be no advance in the language. There would be only a shift within a vast body of linguistic terms already given and complete prior to all possible changes within the language.

On the basis of the discrimination of three kinds of elements, the line, "The greenish quaverings of day" can be analyzed as follows. "Greenish" regarded as an antecedent element means the conventionally accepted meaning of a specific color discriminable on a color chart. "Quaverings" regarded as an antecedent element means shaking, trembling, or trilling. "Day" means the time between sunrise and sunset, or twenty-four hours correlated with the rotation of the earth.

When these terms are regarded as constituents, they function together internally. From this perspective, they are not amenable to translations. They are not abstractable from the line. However, this internal functioning is the basis for discrimination of the terms as consequent elements. Regarded in this way, "Greenish" may be taken to mean what is somewhat unhealthy and mysterious in tone. "Quaverings" means variations or deviations in experience. "Day" means rhythmic periods of conscious life with overtones of fortune, good and bad. Because of the constitutive function of the terms and the origination of new untranslatable meanings, these consequent meanings accrue to the terms of the metaphor.

There are two features of metaphorical expressions that are highlighted by this analysis. The first feature is internal to the boundaries of metaphorical meaning. The antecedent elements relate to each other in an opposition. Literally there are not (or were not) days that quaver or trill. Periods of time do not trill. The antecedent elements clash, and because of their opposition, the metaphor exhibits a negative quality. With respect to this kind of negativity, metaphorical expressions are most clearly illustrated in the oxymoron. The most intense metaphors, the extreme cases, are oxymorons, illustrated by terms such as "the cool heat of imagination," "sweet sorrow," "a wise fool." There is no conventional identity of meaning signified by these terms taken in juxtaposition. Similarly, there is no identity to which we can look in order to effectively compare trills with days – unless we recognize an identity constituted by the inner or internal relations of the terms which initially are understood as antecedent elements, but which are subsequently understood as constituents. When the terms function as constituents, they affect one another. And their interaction is the basis for extracting the terms and regarding them as consequent elements.

Consideration of the oxymoron as archetypal of metaphorical expression brings to the fore the way the antecedent elements clash. The opposition sets the requirements and the possibilities that operate and are generated within the integration of constituents. The opposition within the relation of antecedent elements marks the boundaries of the inner range of meaning of the metaphor. The clash sets the stage for the constituted meanings.[17] Moreover, the greater the intensity of the oppo-

[17] Albert Rothenberg holds a view similar to this. He argues on the basis of both his own experimental studies and analyses of poems that creative acts include "Janus-

sition, the richer the possibilities of the enframed range of meaning. The clash of established intelligibilities breaks the bonds of repetitive and schematic frames of reference. Conventional conceptual perspectives are broken, and meanings are freed for different functions. The sharper the clash, the wider the possibilities of difference. If a contradiction in logic implies all things, a metaphorical tension suggests at least an extensive cluster of meanings that are forthcoming. The contrast between "cool" and "heat" in "the cool heat of imagination" offers diametrically divergent directions or strands of meanings that modify "imagination." The function of these terms as constituents exhibits the intensity of depth and richness now attributable (consequently) to the powers of imagination.

The strength of the clash of a metaphor which is or which approximates an oxymoron, however, is not a condition of absolute openness to constitutive meanings. The oxymoron is not a logical contradiction – everything does not follow. Though the terms as antecedent elements are opposites, they are determinate. The linkages of their determinate antecedent strands of meaning react with one another, for the strands are together in an expression that is not nonsensical, as for instance, the expression, "belated the and trap" is. There is a clash here, too, but the clash is superficial, evident in the joining of terms in an order and context that sets no framework, no matter how broad. The bonds of schematic form are broken, but the break does not lead to constitutive interaction. But the clash between "cool" and "heat" leaves open interaction, particularly in the attribution of these to imagination. Similarly, the terms "greenish" and "quavering," the joining of which approximates the condition of an oxymoron, bring strands of meaning together that can interact constitutively with the strands of meaning of "day."

In addition to the internal negativity of the clash of antecedent elements – which may be called a horizontal negating, since the clash is between accepted meanings – there is a negative aspect of metaphorical expressions regarded as wholes. When regarded as constitutive and as the basis for the extraction of consequent elements, the metaphor negates the world of meanings identifiable in antecedently established contexts. This is a vertical negating, since the clash is between the past that is intelligible and an enhanced present and future of intelligible meanings that give the tradition of language new heights. The metaphor is vertically in opposition to past contexts of meanings articulated conventionally as well as to meanings

ian thinking" or mental processes in which opposition of images or attributes condition the key ingredients of poetic achievements: "The Process of Janusian Thinking in Creativity," *Archives of General Psychiatry*, 24 (1971), 195-205.

formerly exhibited metaphorically (and perhaps mythically). This tension is focused not within antecedent elements but through the opposition between antecedent elements together and merged so as to be transformed into constituents which are projective and amenable to extraction as consequent elements. The vertical negating function of metaphorical expression is what I shall refer to by the term "constitutive negation."

What I have said about the way metaphors are constitutive negations is applicable *mutatis mutandis* to creation in non-verbal media. I shall not here develop this application, since my main purpose is to propose a way in which creativity is intelligible in terms of metaphorical expression. Suffice it to say that paintings which are creations exhibit contrasts in visual qualities and meanings which enframe new intelligibilities – new meanings constituted through contrasts of pictorial and formal elements such as in the compression of representational significance in visual forms as well as in the interplayings of abstract shapes; musical compositions exhibit tensions in melodic lines, harmonic structures, qualities of sounds; architectural creations exhibit contrasts in space; etc. The development of an account of inner or vertical negativity in the various art forms is the subject of another work appropriate to applied aesthetics.

In any case, the discrimination of the elements that comprise a metaphor which is a constitutive negation offers a basis for interpreting the role of creations in the history of a tradition. Antecedent elements are drawn from the tradition and serve as the materials for the forming of the new meaning. The constitutive components function so that the creation is a model for the future. Because of the function of the constituents, the expression yields its unique character, an identity that insists on its new presence in the tradition. Because of this new identity, the consequent elements can function as ingredients in future creations. Thus, they are constitutive in the development of the tradition, and interpretations of works in the tradition depend upon the consequent elements of the metaphor.

4. *Metaphors and "Family Resemblances"*

It will perhaps be helpful at this point to compare what has been said about intelligibility in created objects with Wittgenstein's notion of "family resemblances." At the risk of distorting and misusing Wittgenstein's notion, I shall briefly propose a way in which the interrelations of meanings in metaphors, with certain qualifications, suggests a comparison with the relations among characteristics in a family resemblance. In turn, family resemblances may be compared with the exhibited structures and exemplified Forms of creations.

An obvious qualification of this proposal is that metaphors, at least when they are new, are not general terms as are those for which the notion of family resemblance is useful. Thus, I need not say I agree with the claim that no general terms are definable with reference to essential characteristics or common properties. On the contrary, I believe that some concepts – and I have in mind empirically meaningful concepts which are not arbitrarily or conventionally defined – can be understood by reference to common properties. Indeed my affirmation of structure and Form commits me to this belief. I do not think it follows from the observation that a family does not have one or more characteristics common to all its members that there is no unitary meaning for a family. At minimum, the application of a single term to all its members, however open and flexible this application may be, and however vague the boundaries of the family characteristics may be, suggests that there is an identity that serves as a criterion (though admittedly a partially indeterminate criterion) for identification and knowledge of the family. The meaning may be shown in the way the family name is used. But this does not contradict the claim that a meaning serves as the basis for the use of the name. Moreover, if it is claimed that our inability to discern a property common to all members of the family leads to the conclusion that there is no "hidden" essential nature of the family, then this claim is a philosophical thesis, and not merely the result of the analysis of language.[18] In any case, however this issue

---

[18] The denial of "hidden" essential natures is a philosophical thesis which seems to be influenced by the empiricist tradition and which takes as its model of essential nature an Aristotelean concept of essence. The thesis proposes that, when we *look* and *see* (rather than simply insist that there *must* be something common to all of the members of a family), we fail to find a property common to all members and that we should therefore conclude that there is not a unitary meaning. But this is a thesis which advises us to abandon philosophical reflection. This advice is based upon the conviction that we are misled because we do not recognize the limitations of our demands – demands that there be an ideal that justifies thought and speech. But the norm we are told to use (looking and seeing) is not the only model of philosophical inquiry, or if he intended to reject philosophy in all of its possible forms, then what he says about our being misled on his terms is not relevant to my proposal. My proposal follows from special (philosophical) purposes and consequently I am permitted, even on Wittgenstein's terms, to draw boundaries on the expectation of inquiry. I submit that a Platonic concept of Form, which is not equivalent to the concept of universals or of common properties and which I have proposed in the first chapter of this book, can be proposed as a counter-thesis that provides at least the basis for an account of why a single term is applicable to a range of items which manifest a network, or a cluster, of resemblances. To be sure, the Form cannot be seen with the eyes, any more than can a family as distinct from its members, but its not being seen does not establish its not being cognizable.

may (or may not) be resolved, the purpose of appealing to the notion of family resemblance is not to affirm it as a view about meaning in general but is to use the notion because of its suggestiveness for the view of metaphor I have proposed.

In their metaphorical function, as constituent components, complexes of terms constituting metaphors do not connote articulatable single meanings or sets of characteristics that are common to or implied by the conventional meanings of the antecedent elements. No one coherent set of meanings is common to the totality of meanings of the antecedent elements. Similarly, no one common meaning or set of meanings comprises the whole of an interpretation of a metaphor through extraction of consequent elements. A metaphor presents a complex of familiar meanings which, as constituent components, connect with one another in strands, no one of which is common to the whole of the meaning of the metaphor. Further, since the accepted meanings, or the antecedent elements, make up a combination that appears as incoherent, these meanings are necessarily brought together in broken connections – in connections that exhibit contrast as well as strands of common ingredients. The differences within the cluster of antecedent elements contribute to the functioning of the parts as constituents. Finally, the metaphorical meaning is not equated with the network of articulated antecedent meanings that serves as its necessary condition. In this sense, the metaphor is an instance of linguistic activity that is comparable to that which brings together resemblances like those of a family.

As seen earlier, "winged words" brings together the meanings, swiftness, lightness, flight, and loftiness, among others, with communication, utterance, and articulate expression. No one of the totality is a characteristic common to all. And no one is essential to the unique meaning of the whole. Yet each contributes as it connects with others so as to indicate the whole meaning. Some of the meanings that are attached to one of the explicit terms ("winged") may bear limited common ground with meanings that attached to the other term ("words"). Neither flight nor utterance, attributable to "winged" and "words" respectively, are physical objects. Both are common to the extent that flying takes place through and by virtue of air, and uttering depends upon breath and also takes place through the air. However, the common element of being connected with air does not specify the other meanings of the terms, nor does it give the basis for the interaction of the two terms that give rise to other meanings. Flight can be swift, but swiftness is not necessarily common to loftiness and height. Nor does being winged necessarily mean flying high, with loftiness. Yet when "winged" is joined with "words," loftiness and height are suggested, and this by virtue of the contrast between what it is to be a word conventionally and what it is to be winged. The cluster of meanings that contribute to the metaphor, then, is the basis of an identity and meaning of the whole metaphorical meaning which relates to its conditions as a "family resemblance" relates to its family of characteristics.

There are, as I suggested above, several important qualifications of the notion of family resemblance when it is used to indicate the way metaphorical expression presents new meaning. These qualifications highlight the special way in which metaphors are examplars of created products. First, the term family resemblance does not suggest the importance of the negative aspect of the cluster of antecedent elements that contribute to the metaphor. This negative aspect is explicit and sharp in the connections among antecedent elements. A metaphor does not, like a family resemblance, point to a class of things already recognizable as relevant to one another and comprehended by a single term or complex of terms, such as "game," "language," "human beings" – or "art," for that matter. On the contrary, a metaphor's meaning suggests that incompatible things are connected. Whatever is known to be compatible among the explicit terms or antecedent elements is subordinate to the clash, for the combination of terms implies that although the familiar meanings may have some common elements, these common elements are not relevant to the primary meaning which is suggested by the discordant juxtaposing of the terms.

This point suggests that what warrants referring to a single meaning is not family resemblances but had better be thought of as family character. Indeed, the term "resemblance" is associated with what Wittgenstein's notion of family resemblances is intended to avoid, similarities that cover a multiplicity, which is to suggest that family resemblances are identities that comprehend (and overcome) dissimilars, or differences. But the point of using the notion of family resemblances is to give greater weight to the differences. The term "resemblance," I think, suggests the contrary. In any case, the application of the notion of family resemblance to metaphors, or to created products in general, must be qualified so as to emphasize differences, differences so sharp that they appear as clashes and tensions.

It is significant that such differences can be discerned in families. Whatever it may be that accounts for the application of the same term to all members of a family, there must be room for differences among its members which at once differentiate and sustain the family so that the term for it is still applicable. Moreover, in the case of metaphor, it is the differences which establish the family and which give it its unique status as a family.

A second qualification of family resemblances that must be noted is that the resemblance or family character in question does not cover a multiplicity of examples to which the metaphor applies. It is not a concept embracing a variety of members which connect in strands of resemblances. The new meaning of the metaphor, though an identity, is also singular. Only later, if the metaphor is dead, or if it has become part of conventional language, can it, as a family in relation to its elements, be seen as entering other families and covering more than one instance or applying to a multiplicity of members. But in its newness the family is constituted as a whole; thus, ideally, it is closed. Members cannot pass in and out of its jurisdiction without changing it. And even though some members may be less important than others – the loss of a second cousin would change a family less than the loss of a brother – the members of a fresh metaphor, a creation, function together uniquely so as to constitute a new family. For the moment, no further members are needed, and additional members would detract from it. Only with this constitution, could it be a new model that contributes to the advancement of a tradition – to future "families." And only then can it, once constituted, be open to comprehending future members, or instances in a tradition that has been and will be further advanced.

C. METAPHORS AND THE INTELLIGIBILITY OF CREATED OBJECTS

If this account of metaphor is accepted, we can now address the central question that initiated the proposal that metaphors are models of created objects. In what way is the family character of a metaphor intelligible?

Metaphors and families do seem to be intelligible. We recognize and understand them in some sense. We know their meanings. Moreover, the structure of a metaphor and its intelligibility serves as a model for the intelligibility of created objects. With this in mind, I should next like to explore the question of the intelligibility of metaphors or created objects with respect to their structure.

This topic can be considered at two levels, one specific and the other general. The general problem concerns the possibility that the structure of metaphorical language suggests a model of intelligibility that can be contrasted with the criteria of intelligibility which have dominated the rationalist tradition. It also concerns the possibility of understanding creativity in general. The specific problem concerns the extent to which metaphorical expressions can illuminate or aid in our understanding of individual instances of creativity in their uniqueness. The specific problem will be treated first because a consideration of how specific metaphors exemplify creativity, or more precisely, Novelty Proper, should help to determine the general issue, how metaphorical expression provides a basis for proposing a model of intelligibility appropriate to understanding a world that includes radical creativity.

1. Metaphorical Expression and Paradox

It was said earlier that metaphorical language affords a way to speak appropriately when addressing the problem of understanding creativity. It was also said that the approach to novelty through metaphor encounters the sort of arationality that is present in spontaneity. This is to imply that if a metaphor is a creation, it manifests its own novelty. As an instance of created achievement, it exhibits a unique and distinct individual meaning. Thus, it is necessarily different from all other instances of novelty. How, then, can it illuminate or show the intelligibility of another instance of novelty? How can an expression be helpful in interpreting a created product when the interpretive expression is no more rational than the expression or phenomenon which is to be interpreted?

This problem can be most easily seen in the field of art. One work of art cannot be substituted for another. No play by Shakespeare, for example, can be replaced by another (no matter how similar they might seem in certain respects). A critic attempting to communicate his "understanding" of an art object should not consider his analysis or his impressionistic observations (perhaps his metaphorical expression about it) as equivalent to the original object. Each creation, each metaphor, is an individual archetype, and what models itself after the archetype is derivative. If a metaphor manifests novelty and exemplifies a unique Form, then it cannot repeat, or serve either as a substitute for or a translation of another instance of novelty. Consequently, in exhibiting novelty, a metaphorical expression constitutues a barrier between itself and other examples of novelty.

However, there is a way in which the intelligibility of a created product can be approximated by another creation. A metaphorical expression may make it possible to approach what might be called a "recreation" of created objects. In order to achieve this, a critic of the creation to be understood must be creative. A creative critic, bent on showing the meaning of a created object, for example, may construct his own work of art in the form of a complex metaphor that indicates the original creation in its originality more clearly than could any non-created expression. This is possible, first, because the critic's metaphors, unlike instances of ordinary, "literal" language, resort to violations of familiar patterns of speech. In this way, they reflect the radical aspect and kind of structure of the creation to be understood. Secondly, though the critic's creation may be just as radically novel as the original, it also springs from his grasp of the original, and in this way it embraces the original as a part. The part it appropriates is a complex of consequent elements drawn from the original. There is, of course, an inevitable introduction of interpretive elements in the critic's statements. Yet the kind of criticism that is relevant here is not designed primarily to interpret, but to exhibit the original created object. Whatever interpretations do enter the critical statement, these would be subordinate and instrumental to such exhibiting of the creation.

A successful critic can at least bring the object of criticism into integration with other elements in his own creation; he can bring into focus and, through an interplay with other terms in his expression, display meanings relevant to the object of criticism. A music critic analyzing a Beethoven symphony, for instance, may construct a complex metaphor in verbal language which, as metaphor, is creative. This will not and cannot be a duplication of the symphony. But his words can focus on the symphony, extracting its consequent elements, compressing their meanings and illuminating the object of criticism as a subject that serves as a central element in his own creative, metaphorical expression. Thus, if metaphorical expressions are intelligible to us, specific instances of novelty may be rendered intelligible through the structure which metaphors exhibit. Through metaphorical language, it is possible to exhibit something that approximates the intelligible meanings of examples of novelty.

2. *The Structure of Novelty*

The major purpose in considering metaphorical expression has been to suggest a general model for understanding creativity. It is necessary, then, to extend our consideration of how specific instances of novelty are illuminating to a consideration of establishing a model for making creativity in general intelligible. The first step in this direction already has been taken when it was said that metaphors exhibit the structure of novelty. It should be clear that what is here called the structure of novelty is more precisely the structure of objects that are instances of Novelty Proper – and, in turn, if value is introduced, instances of created objects. The structure of novelty, then, must be seen in the interconnection of those aspects of created objects which specifically make possible the manifestation of Novelty Proper.

The way in which metaphors show the structure of created objects was anticipated by our earlier characterization of creative acts and the arationality of spontaneity. It was pointed out that spontaneity manifests itself as a disruption within the world insofar as the world is a system of determinate events and objects existing in accord with enduring patterns. Novelty occurs where there are discontinuities. But these discontinuities are not simply the differentiation among particular, discrete things. Nor are the discontinuities simply the kinds of distinctions that may be pointed out between all causes and efects or productive agents and their products, such as the difference between antecedent conditions and the effects of these, or between the artist and the work of art produced by him. The discontinuities that must reside in the world in order to make room for spontaneity are discontinuities that are radical; they are not simply differences, but they occur as gaps within otherwise continuous processes. They are gaps within established uniformities; and they must be breaks which are unprecedented, which are contrary to what is expected and demanded by what went before them.

Now the account of metaphorical expressions also referred to discontinuities in rational patterns. Metaphors constitute breaks in conceptual understanding by virtue of their pitting concepts or rationally understood meanings against one another: they present us with what is not the case, with what appears at first blush to deny what we expect of reality. Their function as metaphors is exercised through a tension or opposition which calls attention to a strain placed upon rational categories and which thereby negates the past.

Thus, one characteristic of the structure of novelty is the tension that is manifest initially within the presentation of unexpected relations of meanings and the accompanying negation by the whole metaphor of its past. The unexpectedness, however, should not be thought of as only psychological. We need not at first feel an emotion of surprise at the unexpectedness of the tension. Nor need we interpret what is unexpected as only something which we did not predict. The unexpectedness of the metaphor is more like inconceivability than unpredictability – inconceivability with respect to the demand of the spectator for coherence with his established conceptual perspective toward that which is deemed rational. The initially unexpected tension manifest in instances of novelty, of course, is one of the conditions of the puzzling character of creativity. It is integral to what seems to be the unfamiliarity of what is utterly new.

Negativity, however, is not the only crucial aspect of the structure of novelty. Although a metaphor exhibits something negative, it is also a constituion of a new meaning, a new meaning that has its own identity and a positive, determinate character in its own right. It is this constitutive aspect that shows the break in intelligible order to be more than the sheer absence of continuity. The new product not only exhibits something (a structure) that "rejects" the past, but it also exhibits and thus reveals something that is intelligible. Moreover, in the case of a new product that is a creation, it makes a contribution to the world.[19] Creativity is at once an act of negating the past and an act of affirming a result which contributes to the world. The result, as new, helps to constitute the world in a way that denies what went before it. As was said of metaphors, a creation consists in what we may call "constitutive negation."

If creativity yields a product which, as novel, is constitutive, what more can be said about this constitutive side? Another glance at metaphors will be helpful in answering this question. In negating, metaphors constitute new meaning. The components of the elements are related so that they attain significance only insofar as they are not interpreted in their familiar senses. They must be seen as components that function as constituents. In their capacities as constituting the metaphor, the meanings of the components of the metaphor are regarded as meaning something different from what they are as antecedent elements.

If the concepts that specify meanings in their usual capacity do not yield a coherent result when they are united, the metaphorical expression would be nonsense. But a metaphor is not nonsense. It offers itself as something to be understood, and to be understood, the complex must exhibit unconventional meaning. It requires us to transform attention from familiar to unfamiliar yet intelligible meaning. How can unconventional, unfamiliar meaning be presented as something intelligible? Why is it not just something unfamiliar and unrecognizable?

3. *Intelligibility and Familiarity*

Instances of novelty through contrasts and tensions exhibit meanings which, as both unprecedented and unexpected, appear to us as utterly

[19] The *way* in which it may be a contribution and the *time* when it will be so accepted poses a problem. But, as argued in the first chapter, the characterization of

new. And as utterly new, they are unfamiliar.[20] Yet metaphors, like works of art, present meanings which, though unfamiliar, are after all intelligible. When we apprehend them aesthetically, we understand them in some sense. And the foundation of this understanding can be seen in a feature of metaphorical expression that has been implicit throughout the discussion. At the same time that they are unfamiliar, they have a kind of familiarity. Because of this familiarity in unfamiliarity, aesthetic understanding serves as a second model of intelligibility – a model appropriate to understanding creativity.

Before considering the familiarity of what is utterly new, let me first reiterate my point about the way creations seem unintelligible. As suggested in connection with metaphor, the unexpected quality of a constitutive negation lies not simply in its having been unpredicted, but also in its arational character. From the perspective of what was intelligible, what is new is inconceivable. The inconceivability of novelty is brought into focus in the description of the internal structure of the created object. For we can now see that the tension manifest in what is created is two-fold; it is an opposition among definite, discriminable, conceptualizable elements, and it is an opposition between the antecedent elements in their context and those same elements transformed or reconstituted within the structure constitutive of the total created object.

The two-fold tension in creations is an indispensable condition for what has been taken as unfamiliarity. As the negation of what was known and familiar, novelty makes its appearance as something unfamiliar. And insofar as it presents something which is utterly new, it appears to be totally unfamiliar. In this way novelty seems to be not only arational for our general conceptual understanding of the world, but also utterly unintelligible. Not only can it not be explained, but it cannot be identified. We could only come to know it by effecting our own radical break with our own familiar world. But then the problem of making intelligible our own break, our novelty of response, would arise to take the place of the first problem.

Because of this problem, writers are not always consistent with their initial convictions that novelty is the mark of what appears for the first time. They demand that the newness of created objects be intelligible and

---

creativity is here taken to hinge on the claim that creations contribute to the future – that they are somehow positively valuable, whatever interpretation we give to "value."

[20] Eliseo Vivas, for example, in *The Artistic Transaction and Essays on Theory of Literature* (Columbus: Ohio State University Press, 1963), in particular, pp. 47-48, views the utterly new as something unfamiliar to the spectator.

think it therefore necessary to weaken the definition of novelty by saying that what is new is not utterly new and thus that the created object does not occur as a radical break with its past.

However, once the definition of novelty is weakened in this way, we place ourselves in the hands of the determinist or continuitist who reminds us that his presupposition about the world is, after all, the alternative we must accept in order to avoid the consequence that the created object cannot be rendered intelligible. If the new is continuous (no matter how thin the thread of continuity) with conditions in its past, then it is not literally or radically new. It must be a product in some way linked to the previously known world. All discriminable determinations are increments within the continuity and must connect with one another in accordance with the principle of continuity. "New" additions are simply increments connected with their past. But if there is no increment of the new object which is not traceable to its past, then we have left no room for novelty in the sense of that which is unpredictable and inconceivable in terms of past knowledge. And, most important, we have left no room for growth that is not prefigured in an antecedent world.

A mediating view such as I have affirmed earlier might be thought to assuage the difficulty. We can say that creations are utterly new but not unfamiliar after they have been studied. Creations are not traceable to the past as the past was known prior to the advent of the new. Rather, they are linked to the past as known after the appearance of the creation. The new as an increment enhances knowledge and expands what is conceivable. Thus the new, after its advent, modifies and reconstitutes what was familiar and thereby retains a continuity with the (new) past which becomes familiar in different ways. However, while the view seems to admit the possibility of newness that advances and contributes to the world, it does not succeed in avoiding the problem. This problem reappears in the relation between the two pasts that are blurred in order to save continuity and the need for familiarity. The two pasts, simply, are the past past, or the past as previously intelligible, and the new past, or the past as newly intelligible. If these are continuous, then the new is after all wholly traceable to the past as previously known. But if novelty is introduced so as to modify the previously intelligible past, and if the outcome is not merely the reshuffling of the elements of this past past, then the outcome or new past breaks in some way with that past past. And this break marks the advent of something radically unfamiliar, even if one can later see its coherence with the new past. Must we admit, then, that the created object in its newness is utterly unfamiliar and therefore ultimately unintelligible? In short, must we conclude that the unique meaning in that which is new is after all fundamentally unintelligible?

At this point, the special relation of the unprecedented and unconceptualizable aspect of created objects to their unfamiliarity must be brought into sharper focus. When it is said that what is utterly new is unfamiliar and unintelligible, it is assumed that being familiar is dependent upon being expected and conceptualizable. This assumption must be challenged. Neither being expected nor being conceivable is identical with being familiar. For example, a familiar friend may call on us unexpectedly. That he is unexpected does not mean that he is either unfamiliar or unintelligible. Moreover, a friend, at least if he is an intimate acquaintance, is not fully conceptualizable, though he is not therefore deemed unfamiliar. There is something about an acquaintance that eludes rational categories and that includes an ineffable character which is nevertheless quite familiar, though unconceptualizable. What is known by acquaintance is in some sense intelligible. An acquaintance is an immediately coherent presentation – a subject of attention – that is manifest and familiar to the one who is acquainted. An acquaintance is recognizable and, in a non-discursive way, identifiable. An acquaintance is an indubitable *datum* which is open for acceptance and affirmation. We do not look perceptually or conceptually for such a datum. But we do approach such a datum cognitively.[21]

Can we say, however, that novelty is familiar in the way an acquaintance is? Have we not defined novelty as that which is unlike all that went before it? Is not novelty unfamiliar precisely because we are unacquainted with it? If so, it seems that the newness of a created object is, after all, unfamiliar and unintelligible. The possibility of avoiding this admission is crucial to the proposal that metaphors serve as models of the intelligibility of creations. Whether we can avoid admitting that newness is necessarily unfamiliar hinges on whether we are willing to grant that something can appear to us as familiar on first sight. Some acquaintances, on our first encounter with them, do appear as things or persons we recognize. They are manifest, open, demanding attention, *as if* they were familiar from past experience. But they are initially familiar and recognizable, not by previous acquaintance or previous knowledge, but by an immediate acknowledgement. They appear as the unexpected which should have

---

[21] The claim that there are ineffable but familiar and intelligible objects of awareness is not new. It has been made by many others of widely varying philosophical persuasions. It is found, for instance, in the notion of concrete experience in Idealism and in the concept of knowledge by acquaintance in Russell. But it is a kind of awareness that we sometimes overlook in our quest for conceptual intelligibility.

been expected, as the unfamiliar (in terms of prior familiarities) which at once is familiar.

This phenomenon is found in art and has, indeed, already been indicated by our consideration of the way metaphors present something unfamiliar, but which nevertheless demands acknowledgement. The structure and meaning of the metaphor, or more generally, the art object, though new and unfamiliar with respect to the past, calls forth our attention in such a way that we recognize the structure as that which should have been there – as that which the context of what is present within the work demanded but which we did not and could not recognize before. Thus a musical composition by Mozart presents an inevitable order, a painting by Cézanne exhibits a complex of color masses that could not have been otherwise, a drama by Shakespeare shows a progression of action that must be as we find it.[22] The inevitability of such presentations is the condition for there being some objective or, minimally, shared meanings. Interpretations, to be sure, may diverge, but the agreements we do find, and the possibility for disagreement about works of art, depend upon acknowledgement of some focus that functions as an identity to which various interpretations are relevant or irrelevant.

In the case of metaphorical expressions, what is encountered are parts functioning as constituents. This functioning and the constituents themselves appear as immediately familiar. They present themselves for immediate acquaintance. They are presented in the context of a structure that is also contrasted with antecedent continuities and extractable antecedent elements. Hence, the constituents are apprehended as over against what is conceptualizable and with which a discontinuity is exhibited. Further, the structure is analyzable into consequent elements, and these are apprehended by virtue of an acquaintance with constituents exhibiting the new meaning – a new meaning, familiar by acquaintance, that provides the basis for the consequent elements. Our understanding of the consequent elements reveals that there is also an immediate understanding of the constitutents. Finally, the constituents presented in contrast with antecedent elements are apprehended as transformations of what was antecedent. Change is integral to the way the structure appears to cogni-

---

[22] If someone were to object that such experiences are illusory, that we only feel the necessity – a Freudian interpretation might, for example, attribute the sense of unprecedented familiarity to unconscious conditions – then he must deny the place of these experiences in the world for much the same reasons offered by the determinist. It would then be necessary for him to explain away these subjective, illusory experiences of familiarity and necessity as unreal occurrences in our lives. And his explanation would lead to the puzzles discussed in the second chapter.

tion. The new structure is given as a complex of familiar meanings manifest in evolutionary change – from past familiarity through unfamiliarity to new familiarity.

This suggestion that Novelty Proper offers itself as immediate, underived, and somehow familiar as well as unfamiliar, points to the possibility of regarding creativity as intelligible in accord with a second way of understanding – a way that serves as model of intelligibility which is especially appropriate to the paradoxical advent of created objects. In the next chapter I shall reaffirm the need for such a model and for a perspective that brings together this model with the standards of discursive and conceptual intelligibility.

CHAPTER IV

FUNDAMENTAL PARADOX AND INTELLIGIBILITY

INTRODUCTION

From the beginning, I have insisted that creations and the acts which lead to them appear to be paradoxical intrusions within an otherwise intelligible world. I have offered reasons for accepting such intrusions as irreducible increments in a potentially intelligible system of things and events. But I have also suggested a way in which creations may themselves be intelligible in spite of their paradoxical relation to their contexts. If creations are intelligible presentations for immediate acquaintance, then, even though paradoxical, they can be regarded as intelligible components of reality. In turn, spontaneity, which is manifest as discontinuities that precede new and conceptually unfamiliar products, may be understood to the extent that these discontinuities are relevant to non-conceptually identifiable structures. However, the acknowledgement of non-conceptual as well as conceptual intelligibility raises a fundamental issue: What is the relationship between non-conceptual intelligibility and conceptual understanding? How can both ways of understanding together comprise our understanding of the world? This larger issue cannot be avoided in a discourse which insists that from the perspective of conceptual understanding creations are radical and paradoxical and that these are nevertheless intelligible in another way. If both claims are to be affirmed in a single view, then the relation of the two ways of understanding must be explored. Ignoring this relation would be to ignore an implied epistemological dualism which, whether affirmed or denied, requires further explanation.

An attempt to relate conceptual and non-conceptual intelligibility might be interpreted as an attempt to merge the two models of understanding in a thesis about a final unitary vision of the world. Such a vision, indeed, is an aim that seems to require the topic of this final chapter. But it is an aim which is ideal, and the hope of actualizing this ideal is itself subject to question. With this in mind, I shall try to show that even if we could fit radical creation into such a vision of the world, we could face an even more fundamental increment of unintelligibility in the world. This break in intelligibility occurs as a paradox present at a level of inquiry more basic than that which we see in instances of creativity.

The presence of paradox encountered at this more fundamental level can be introduced through a discussion of the notion of "the absurd." Consideration of "the absurd" as a point of departure extends what has been a study of creativity to an exploration of the more general conditions of understanding the totality of phenomena that comprise a world which is inclusive of spontaneity. This expansion of the topic will lay the basis for a further characterization of the two ways of understanding, each of which presupposes a distinct model of intelligibility. However, in treating the issue in the broader context, our approach takes on a breadth that will not exclude what has been said about the issue as it is encountered in creativity. Rather, it incorporates within a larger context the problems which already have been discussed. The broader perspective to which we now turn should serve as a link between this discourse on creativity and a larger task for the future of proposing an ontology of creativity.

My plan is to begin by discussing what the notion of the absurd means in the context of contemporary thought, *viz.*, that acknowledgement of the absurd depends upon understanding experience in terms of discursive, conceptual standards. I shall then return to the suggestion that on the second model of intelligibility (that which has been found in aesthetic experience), creativity, and likewise the absurd, is manifest as intelligible. But I shall use this suggestion to show how the second model establishes for the finite knower a tension with conceptual intelligibility and leads to the paradox which is even more fundamental than the paradox encountered in creative acts. Finally, I shall discuss the possibility of understanding according to a third model of intelligibility that can affirm this paradox as well as the other two models.

I should point out before proceeding that what I refer to as models of intelligibility are called models with varying degrees of appropriateness. The second kind of intelligibility is most obviously tied to a model, the model of metaphor and aesthetic experience. The standards of the intelligibility in question are disclosed in something concrete. Our recognition of this intelligibility depends upon actual experiences of specific kinds of objects. Metaphors, or aesthetic objects in general, exhibit this intelligibility; response to these objects includes a kind of apprehension that conforms to what in them is intelligible. The standards of intelligibility, then, appear in a model, since they are discerned because intelligibility is first encountered in actual occasions and concrete objects.

In contrast, conceptualization and relational order, which is essential to what I have called the first kind of understanding, is not so clearly dependent upon a kind of concrete presentation. Although the standards of intelligibility may be applicable to singular objects, they are not disclosed by virtue of an understanding of singular objects. On the contrary, understanding of such objects depends upon standards that have a priority in relation to the objects. Intelligibility depends upon standards manifest as invariance or identity, and apprehension of these requires conformance to stringencies, boundaries, and foci rather than actual occasions which exemplify the standards. Yet the terms "stringencies," "boundaries," and "foci" are suggestive of a model. They constitute a cluster of abstract controls. Such controls may be signalized by picturing in visual terms. These controls are most readily describable by means of reference to images of apparently stable physical objects and properties in contrast to changing, unstable states of objects. Things as contrasted with events prompt our recognition of the controls that are made possible by identities which impose stringencies, boundaries, and foci on what is intelligible. In the sense that visible things and events are helpful in calling attention to the standards of understanding in question, the first kind of intelligibility is referred to as a model.

Reference to the standards of the third kind of understanding (if such understanding is possible) is least appropriately thought of as a model. The requirements in this case, it will be seen, are not determinate. But further consideration of this issue must be postponed until later.

A. THE ABSURD

In its most general meaning, the term "absurd" may be applied to what fails to make sense. The failure to make sense occurs under a variety of conditions. For instance, it may occur as something unexpectedly contrary to normal behavior, such as man's laughing at the loss of his most valued possession. It may occur as what is contrary to regularities in phenomena, such as rain's falling from a cloudless sky. Occurrences of absurdity may provoke a range of responses. For instance, absurdity may appear to be foolish, thus provoking laughter. It may provoke terror, as in cases of incongruity in experience that is threatening. Or it may be the condition for an insight into man's relation to the world.

However, whatever our responses to the absurd, there seems to be a common ground for all of its instances. In every case, what is absurd is something that appears to be out of place. There is an incongruity, an inconsistency, a conflict with a context that appears as lawful, orderly experience. As Camus points out, absurdity "springs from a comparison," a comparison between two aspects of reality which seem to be out of harmony.[1]

This notion of absurdity serves as an initial and general characterization that is consistent with current usage. However, in this general form, the notion conceals an important distinction. The distinction may be defined as a contrast between what is absurd and what is a surd. What is absurd is what is only surprising or only temporarily absurd. A surd is irrational in principle. As such, it is what is inevitably and structurally absurd. Rather than use the term "surdity," I shall refer to the inevitably absurd, or the condition of being absurd in principle, as "fundamental absurdity." In contrast, the merely surprising or temporarily absurd will be called the apparently absurd. In apparent absurdity, incongruity ceases to be evident once it is seen in its proper place in an ordered context. A man's laughing at the loss of his most valued possession is no longer incongruous if we find what that his laughing is for him a typical hysterical reaction expressing sorrow. Rain from a cloudless sky can be explained in terms of unusual meteorological conditions, and once we know the explanation, the absurdity vanishes. On the other hand, what is fundamentally absurd resists being made coherent. It defies characterization by means of consistently applied categories.[2]

---

[1] Albert Camus, *The Myth of Sisyphus and Other Essays*, translated by Justin O'Brien (New York: Vintage Books, Alfred A. Knopf, Inc., and Random House, Inc., 1955), "The Myth of Sisyphus," pp. 3-102.

[2] Someone might propose that there is a sense in which every instance of incongruity can be subjected to order. Incongruities can be related to categories, even if only by a purported principle of contrast between disorder and order. All occurrences of what fails to make sense, then, in principle, would be amenable to some sort of order, an order by which we construe the world as, after all, rational. If one insists on this, then all instances of the absurd are construed as apparent. In response, it should be made clear that what is at issue here concerns the kind of order imposed on experience and the way absurdity is or is not amenable to it. I admit that all occasions of absurdity can be related to an order in at least one way. We can view such occasions as rationally comprehended negations within rationality and thereby claim to have imposed upon them the order of a negative relation. But this does not imply that all incongruities are therefore only temporary or apparent. For there are some tensions that are not resolvable within themselves, no matter what larger relation embraces them. Some occurrences cannot be shown to be conceptually understandable in their own constitution as this appears within otherwise ordered continuities. It is this kind of inescapable absurdity, I think, which is the basis for the meaning generally given the term "the absurd." And it is this fundamental absurdity which is taken to be coincident with unintelligibility. To impose on these what is taken to be a negative

The acknowledgement of absurdity, whether apparent or fundamental, is inseparable from the acceptance of the traditional standards of conceptual intelligibility. This model must now be examined. The first and second chapters of this book prepared the way for an examination of conceptual intelligibility. Throughout, the discussion presupposed that intelligibility depends upon conceptualization. In accord with this model, something is intelligible, most generally, if it is self-identical and consequently apprehended as an identity or determinate thing which has connections with other things. The thing which is intelligible must have sufficient determinateness to be identifiable in the midst of differences. As I have emphasized already, intelligibility need not depend on full and complete definiteness. There are degrees of definiteness and thus degrees of determinateness. At its best, the required determinateness would be manifest as definite unity, a complete self-identity that is discernable and precisely identifiable. At the least, the required determinateness is a focus for a togetherness that is recognizable. In any case, in order to be recognizable and identifiable, the determinateness of a thing must be consistent with itself, and, if relevant to a process that is sequentially temporal, the determinateness must be identical and invariant throughout variation. It must be manifest and remain steadfast, as an identity which endures in the midst of change. To be determinate is to be distinct and fixed.[3]

On the model that derives from the tradition, intelligibility requires the presentation of immutable determination, of what can be called "essence" or what I earlier called "Form." The sense of Form here covers both Platonic and Aristotelean views, because the question of the status of Form is not at the moment crucial. I claim only that intelligibility attaches to a repeatable object which is recognized as repeatable because of an invariant, an enduring identity, whether the identity is transcendent or immanent in relation to what it identifies. This model of intelligibility covers the most tough-minded empiricism, which demands consistency, repeatability, and identity in the data which serve as evidence for explanation. Even a narrowly defined nominalism presupposes that intelligibility

---

relation in order to assimilate them to rationality is at least to stop short of specifying a positive framework under which the absurd is perfectly subsumed. Indeed, to view instances of the absurd as bearing a negative relation to the order of the world is to affirm through the acknowledgement of negation that the absurd does oppose the rational framework in which the world is understood.

[3] Intelligibility in this general sense is, I take it, something like what Heidegger, in his essay "Plato's Doctrine of Truth," refers to in discussing the unhiddenness of truth. See "Plato's Doctrine of Truth," translated by John Barlow, in *Philosophy in the Twentieth Century*, Vol. II, edited by William Barrett and Henry D. Aiken (New York: Random House, 1962), pp. 251-270.

depends in some way on identity in difference – on regularity, or something invariant in variation, if only because nominalism requires the consistent use of names. My claim is that the basis of widely variant methodological as well as metaphysically committed views in the tradition lies in the presupposition that what is intelligible must be recognizable by virtue of an identifiable and invariant factor, a factor which will be called "Form."

It is important to notice that intelligibility need not depend on single, uncompounded Forms. In other words, one may deny that singular, simple objects of thought are intelligible independently of contexts. Whether such intelligibility is or is not denied depends on the version of the traditional model of rationality that is adopted. For the moment, I shall assume that there are no intelligible single, simple identities, because I want to discuss the traditional model in its broadest aspects. If what I say applies to this, it should apply to the other version.

Form, then, directly reveals the presence of intelligibility. Form is a condition of understanding. At the same time, Form should not be thought of as a referential sign of intelligibility, for then the Form would be separated from its own intelligibility. Intelligibility is not exhausted by the Forms which reveal it. But neither are Forms separable items that refer to intelligibility. Rather, Forms are the necessary conditions under which intelligibility is present. Without Form intelligibility would not be present. Yet the presence of a Form guarantees neither that understanding gains full intelligibility nor that all that is intelligible is given in the Form. This, I believe, is consistent with what Plato considered crucial in the relation of the Forms to the Good. The Forms lead dialectically to the Good, which in turn is the source of the intelligibility of the Forms.

The suggestion that a Form in itself is not identical with intelligibility points to another requirement that is consistent with, if not affirmed by, the tradition: intelligibility need not be restricted to objects of cognition that are both singular and simple. Thus, a simple Form taken in itself, in isolation, not only could not be the same as intelligibility, but it would not, taken by itself, be fully intelligible. In order that a Form make a thing intelligible, it requires co-present conditions. Such conditions may consist in the instantiation of the Form or in its connections with other Forms. Triangularity, for example, is intelligible by virtue of the Forms of being a straight line and an intersection, of points and angularity, etc. Redness is intelligible in connection with possible instances of the color, red. Further, these conditions as well as the Form in question must have connections that lead to a larger complex or system. This view is the kind for which metaphysical idealism and pragmatism are exemplary.

The point I wish to make is simply that intelligibility is not limited to immediate cognitions of single objects. However, even for those who affirm immediate or first cognition – and consequently single, simple intelligible objects – the intelligibility of such cognitions depends upon a context to which simple cognitive objects are relevant. A Form is not an absolute identity with no relations to what is other than itself. A Form reveals intelligibility by virtue of its having a place in what is purportedly a more comprehensive complex, or a system. Each Form must interlace and connect with others in such a way that some are more basic than others and in such a way that each of them depends upon its relation to an ideal whole. However, I also believe that the model of intelligibility of the tradition implies a requirement that is more fundamental than this demand for connection in a system at first suggests. Indeed, if the intelligibility of a part of the system is based on the system as a whole, intelligibility is also manifest without dependence on a larger context, and it must be acknowledged in a cognitive act that is direct and immediate; for the system or whole must itself reveal an intelligibility of enduring identity in the midst of variation, and this is to function as a single (though complex) Form. The system is intelligible by virtue of its being based on determinateness – that is, on the identity which grounds the connection among the components of the system – which is at bottom a complex but single Form, the Form of the Whole. Conceptual intelligibility, then, requires that Forms in connection compose a complex which functions as a single Form within which connections are present. Further, even if the Whole is conceived as developmental and intelligible in terms of a principle of growth, its unfolding identity must comprehend the moments of this growth as components in a continuum. The idea of a developing system presupposes either that there is an actual culmination that will complete the development or that a completable whole is an ideal limit functioning regulatively with respect to development. Peirce's conception of the reasons for adopting the pragmatic method as well as scientific realism is faced with this issue. The point is that unless one stops short of offering reasons for what is accepted as intelligible, then one cannot avoid acknowledging a systematic whole in some sense. But whether the system as a whole is construed as an ideal or as an actual state to be realized, that whole must manifest the features of Form, of an identity in difference.

Against this model of intelligibility, it is possible to sharpen the view of the absurd under discussion. The demand for the assignment of things and events to a place within a systematic whole is the basis of our recognition of the absurd. The absurd is a violation of the consistency required by systematic order. It is a violation because it is a radical opposition to, rather than merely a deviation from, order. As the incongruous, the inconsistent, or that which is without reason, the absurd manifests unintelligibility in the strong sense that it conflicts with Form. It manifests unintelligibility not simply in occurrences of the unexpected, the surprising, or the puzzling. It is not simply an appearing of the unknown. The unexpected and the unknown may be only apparently absurd. To equate the absurd with the puzzling is to give priority to the knower and to interpret the absence of order as provisional, i.e., as a problem which awaits the power of intellect to overcome it and thus re-establish intelligibility. But the absurd in its fundamental sense is not merely the absence of rationality. Nor is it the unknown remainder of an incomplete construction of Forms in a system. The fundamentally absurd is the unintelligible in principle. It is that which persists in being an incongruity. It cannot be subjected to conceptual explanation because its self-identity is to be in conflict. It is the necessarily unintelligible in that it is what contradicts the presupposition of rational intelligibility. By nature it is unconceptualizable.

Translated in the terms of the model of intelligibility described above, being absurd, or radically unintelligible in the fundamental sense, is to be an inconsistent identity. It is to be the enemy of Form. But, as radical, the fundamentally absurd is also permanent impermanence; it is the inevitable manifestation of inconsistency. Another way of putting this is to say that the fundamentally absurd shows itself as the Formless in essence, which is to say that unlike apparent absurdity, which is simply the absence of Form, the fundamentally absurd is disclosed in the presentation of a "Form," the "Form" of inevitable Formlessness.

B. TWO LOCI OF THE ABSURD

The contexts in which fundamental absurdity is encountered have been the concern of writers who have been most explicit in speaking about absurdity in connection with human existence. Sartre's writing, for instance, contains much that is richly suggestive. In his novel *Nausea*, there are vivid presentations of the awareness of absurdity: for instance, Roquentin's dizzying realization of the elusiveness of self-awareness and his recognition of the contingency and instability of the reality to which he attempts to ascribe stable meanings.[4] In *Being and Nothingness*, when

---

[4] *Nauseau,* translated by Lloyd Alexander (Norfolk, Connecticut: New Directions, 1949).

Sartre speaks of the absolute contingency of human reality, he refers to what I have called the fundamentally absurd.[5] In this work, he points to the most general and deep-rooted conflicting conditions of experience. However, I should like to pursue the question of the loci of absurdity independently of Sartre's view and of any specific approach that might be associated with existential philosophy.

In what contexts or situations, then, can radical unintelligibility occur? There are two kinds of situations which can be singled out: situations in which there are occurrences of spontaneity and situations in which there is explicit manifestation of the relation of human consciousness to conceptual intelligibility. The reason for saying that spontaneity is a locus of the absurd should be obvious. The reason, of course, depends upon what it means for a product to exhibit a new structure or to newly exemplify a Form. As I have argued, an occurrence that newly exemplifies a Form is an instance in which there is a violation of conceptualized patterns as these were known in the world prior to the occurrence of Novelty Proper. Now, this violation of patterns might be construed as temporary and as another instance of the apparently absurd. If it is so regarded, the novel structure is viewed as intelligible in exhibiting a Form that is recognized for the first time, but, because it is discovered to be intelligible, it is taken to be constitutive of the intelligible world which hitherto was not as fully understood. From this perspective, an instance of spontaneity is a revelation that can be conceptualized after the fact. However, the arguments offered earlier should make clear my opposition to the view that spontaneity is an instance of apparent absurdity. These arguments support the view that spontaneity exhibits fundamental absurdity. A new structure is a manifestation of a Form which, though it appears as a discovery, reveals an intelligibility that transforms the intelligibility of the world. This point is a reiteration of what was said earlier about the unfamiliarity of the past which, because of a creation, may be seen in terms of a reconstituted or new past. Unintelligibility, then, is necessarily present in the discontinuity between the intelligibility prior to an instance of spontaneity and new intelligibility revealed by the Form of the new structure. This discontinuity constitutes a tension in the form of an incongruity within intelligibility. Thus, there is an inevitable surd, a fundamental absurdity disclosed in each act that leads to an instance of the radically novel. The fundamentally absurd appears in the gap between the old and the new. Absurdity appears with Novelty Proper, and it reveals the necessary inadequacy of attempts to achieve a complete conceptual scheme based on the traditional model.

[5] *Being and Nothingness, An Essay on Phenomenological Ontology, op. cit.*

This account of the locus of fundamental absurdity in creative acts raises a basic problem that was acknowledged in the first chapter (pp. 33-35). Although adequate treatment of this problem requires the development of an ontology of creativity, I should like to digress briefly in order to adumbrate the kind of approach I believe is necessary. The relevance of the problem in the context of this chapter is different from its relevance earlier, since here we are concerned with intelligibility in general rather than a description of the way creations appear to be new.

The problem centers on the question whether Forms exemplified for the first time are not only independent of, but are also antecedent to, the structures that exemplify them. It seems appropriate to conclude that if they are antecedent, then spontaneity would be excluded from the complex of Forms that makes the world intelligible. Spontaneity would be an appearance, relegated to what is temporal, and, with respect to Form, it is derivative for intelligibility. Creativity, then, would be acknowledged to occur in time, but a fully realized understanding of it would provide a system which, on the basis of atemporal necessities requires all sequences of derived events in which temporal novelty occurs. At bottom the issue turns on the relation of structure to Form. The notion of structure as immanent focuses the contrast between what is, on the one hand, atemporal and intelligible and, on the other hand, what is temporal and only apparent, or what is dependent upon the temporal. As exhibited in concrete objects, structures come into existence and cease to exist. Forms are not exhibited, and they are not dependent on the contingencies of individual existents that come and go. If they could in some sense come into being, they would not therefore come into existence. But it is problematic whether they come into being in any sense, for coming into being requires time, and Forms transcend temporality. The only way to speak to this problem, while insisting on novelty at the level of Forms, is, I think, to affirm the possibility of discontinuity at the level of Forms. The kind of discontinuity possible must be found in deviant ways in which hierarchies of Forms are ordered, and in an admitted dissociation of certain Forms from one another in a system that is incomplete. A more complete account of such a system is the subject of an ontology of creativity. However, it is essential here to observe that whatever the details of an ontology that is open to two levels or domains in which novelty has a place – the domain of atemporal being and the domain of temporal existence – a paradox is inevitable. The paradox is focused in the relation of the timeless and the existent in time. It is this relation which is sharply evident in the second locus of fundamental absurdity.

The second locus of the absurd is seen in the contrast between the criteria traditionally associated with intelligibility and the activity of knowing. If intelligibility depends upon the manifestation of identity, it also demands that the knower be oriented correctly toward the known. Cognition must be adequate to its object, and to be adequately oriented, knowing must occur in a relation that endures and stabilizes the act of knowing in accord with the stability of the identity of the intelligible object. To think about triangularity requires an accommodation of thought to invariant identities of points, lines, and angles in relation. Thought must fix itself on its object. The consistency and permanence that are ideally necessary to the presence of intelligibility could only be met by an intellect which is as stable as the object to which it should be adequate. The knower must endure as an identity in difference which approximates to the permanence of its object. Thus, not only does Form serve as the model for intelligibility, but it also serves as the model for an intellect that is adequate to its ideal object. Consciousness functioning as intellect, then, must be established in an unchanging determination that conforms to an unchanging, determinate object.[6]

The paradox under discussion focuses on the relation of the act of knowing to the requirements of the object of knowledge. Knowing is a function of human consciousness, and human consciousness has what I

---

[6] It might be argued, as it has been by some naturalists in this country, that knowing is not a special activity undertaken by a special kind of reality, consciousness. There is no distinction in fact between knower and known. Knowing is only one natural event among others. Consequently, acts of knowing are events that give rise to problems no different from those of establishing antecedents and consequents of any event that is the subject of inquiry. In response to this position, it should be pointed out that apart from the issue whether consciousness can be reduced to or understood in terms of public data, the argument does not avoid the puzzle of how the requirements of conceptual intelligibility can be met by a finite and changing inquirer. Even if knowing is called an event, as an event, it is nevertheless bounded in some way, just to the extent that it is one event and not all of experience. Further, as an event, it is temporal and in transition. How, then, can it be understood as adequately or exhaustively correlated with conditions that endure as identities that are not transformed from moment to moment? This question directs attention to an issue not reducible to the issue of correlating regularities with events. For what is in question is an event, knowing, that consists in specifying the very correlations that are supposed to make itself intelligible. How, then, can the identifying event identify itself in its identifying? The only way to avoid this puzzle is to reject entirely the model of conceptual intelligibility and to insist that identity is not what provides intelligibility. Consequently, all standards, so called, would be in flux. This view has been denied earlier. But it is important to see that if it is not denied, no position can be held, no event can be identified as being one kind of thing rather than another, and no standard can stand as a standard. The model of intelligibility suggested by metaphor shares with what I see as the significance of the naturalist's thesis, the recognition of the unavoidability of change. But this second model of intelligibility is not therefore offered as an alternative, but rather as a complementary model to the traditional presupposition of conceptual intelligibility.

shall refer to as existential or (for our purposes here) actual being in contrast to possible or ideal, atemporal being. This is to say that consciousness is finite and, in having a beginning and a terminus, it is both discontinuous and temporal. How, then, can a finite consciousness existing in time achieve the ideal required in order to apprehend changeless Form? Only a consciousness transcendent of the discontinuities in its temporal and finite existence could meet this requirement. Only a divine consciousness could fully measure up to the ideal demands of intelligibility. Surely this was implied by Plato and Aristotle as well as a host of others who followed them. The philosopher is a lover of wisdom. But if he were to reach his goal, he would have died as a human being in love with Form; he would have attained the perfect vision of the unity of all diversity through a union with a permanence that transcends transition.

There is a sense in which Plato's allegory of the cave suggests the point that human consciousness does not, after all, fulfill this ideal. Not only is the prisoner who was once chained dazzled by intelligibility, but after the journey into the sunlight is complete, the soul of the then wise man cannot rest. It returns to the shadows. Even if we accept the argument that this return is the result of force or that it is done against the will of the wise man, we should observe that if the wise man were not finite and human, he would not succumb. Human consciousness is not, after all, divine. It is finite, and its vision cannot abide with ultimate intelligibility. Finite consciousness, then, cannot endure this demand of perfection. It is a perpetually unstable relationship with Form. And to the extent that it approaches the goal of intelligibility, its existence as a temporal and finite being is denied.

The discrepancy between the temporal activity of knowing and its ideal of fully realized intelligibility is illustrated when we encounter frequently repeated exemplifications of a Form. The continued repetition of a word, for instance, leads to a loss of intelligible meaning. Through perpetuation, what is understood is given such emphasis that it loses its power to constitute an identity for consciousness. Only the sound remains; and that too falls into the ludicrous, unless in some way it is captured for aesthetic purposes and thereby given a different status. Similarly, the repetition of a musical figure on a broken record also passes into the ridiculous. What is at first musically intelligible loses its intelligibility for us as it is repeated. I do not think this happens because the repeated sounds consists of a fragment whose whole is lost by virtue of undue emphasis on the fragment. For a whole melody when heard many times in sequence becomes meaningless for finite consciousness. Such examples provide concrete illustration of the incompatibility of finite understanding and perfected intelligibility in a wholly stable system.

The occasion of recognizing the absurd in the relation of consciousness to Form also may be realized in situations in which forms are apprehended without reference to a context that gives "space" for intelligence to "move." For example, unqualified attention to a Form such as triangularity, or to the determinations expressed by the worlds "number" or "ratio," is also an ideal which reveals loss of intelligibility. These, as distinct items of meaning, require a context in which they can have coherence. Only if all such determinations were given place in a system could they be understood perfectly and recognized as fully intelligible.[7]

Consciousness seldom recognizes the absurd as revealed in the relation of itself to Form. Most of us do not normally encounter the absurd in this fundamental manifestation. Rather, we are more comfortable in unreflectively passing from one familiar determination to another familiar determination – from one known Form to another known Form. On rare occasions, however, consciousness does apprehend this source of the absurd. There are moments when the knower is aware of the incongruity of Form and consciousness. These moments are found, for example, in situations in which radical novelty is effected within personality transformations, in moments of moral crisis, and in certain acts of philosophical reflection. But whatever the specific occasions for this manifestation of the absurd, such occasions provide awareness of the peculiarity of the relation of cognitive consciousness to its intelligible object.

Now if conceptual intelligibility could be satisfied, the system itself would need to be stable and undisturbed by intrusion. But consciousness as temporal would inevitably threaten to intrude. Consequently, if finite consciousness is not to violate that to which it strives to conform, and if it were to succeed fully in being adequate to its object, it must vanish as that which envisages the system because it must be an identity in stable connection with its object – which is to be taken up within the system. And this latter alternative would mean that human consciousness must transcend itself and become one with what it is not. Thus, it seems that the

---

[7] Someone might object that these examples do not illustrate loss of intelligibility but rather boredom and loss of attentiveness on the part of the hearer or knower. There is no doubt that in such cases attention wanes. But this does not warrant the conclusion that the hearer can meet the demands of the stability that reveals intelligibility. The weariness of attention itself shows that consciousness is unstable. Whatever the knower's response may be, what is shown is that finite consciousness is inadequate to the task of the intellect in reaching full conceptual intelligibility. Human consciousness fails to remain steadfast and loses adequate contact with intelligibility. And this is inevitable because cognition is effected by consciousness which is temporal.

opposition between the existence of consciousness and the first model of intelligibility could only be overcome by a denial of the existential pole of the opposition.

The opposition would not be avoided by a denial of the other pole. Suppose we insist that we should not impose the requirements of intelligibility on experience. We would not then be responsible for the model of intelligibility presented, and the alleged inadequacy of consciousness to Form would not be necessary. Accordingly, the fashionable view in some circles would point out that the philosophical tradition has misled us and that we are advised to abandon the essentialist model of intelligibility.

It is true that I have said that the absurd depends on the relation of consciousness to its object. And I have indicated that we have inherited the first model of intelligibility from a philosophical tradition. However, cognitive consciousness aimed at the requirement of atemporal intelligibility is rooted in a primordial relationship that is prior to conditions of dependence or independence of the object known on the knower. Although a characterization of consciousness and its place in the world belongs to another study, the point that the relation of consciousness to its object is primordial must be treated briefly in the present context.[8]

Consciousness exists as an intention of objects. It does not exist as an entity or real being that is independent of intentions. It is consciousness precisely as an intending of an object. As such, consciousness is correlative with objects. If consciousness becomes reflexive, it encounters itself in and through awareness of some object. Objects and consciousness are interdependent. In such a relation, the object is sustained. In order to be sustained, it is an identity that endures; otherwise, consciousness would have nothing to intend and would not then exist. But if the object is an identity, it presents the ingredient of the model of intelligibility in which atemporal identity is a requirement. For our immediate purposes, then, it is essential to see that there is an intelligibility attributed to certain objects correlated with consciousness as it functions cognitively. Neither objects nor intelligibility are created by consciousness. They are not its whimsical consequences. Rather, they are given with consciousness, and their identities are required for consciousness in its cognitive function. Yet since cognition is given in an act of consciousness, in a contingent, temporal existent, it

[8] This is not to say that consciousness is indistinguishable from its objects. Nor is it to say that there is no identity or enduring reality other than objects through which consciousness can be apprehended. I think there is present with consciousness an identity, a "self" that is relevant to complexes of intentions and to the transitory existence of consciousness. But a "self" is not one with the existential actuality that functions cognitively. Cognition is conscious activity, and conscious activity takes place at moments in time.

too is finite and approximate with respect to the identity of the object that is given for it.

What has been said about the relationship between finite consciousness and intelligibility does not necessitate a view that intelligibility has a subjective status or that it is the product of consciousness. The acknowledgement of the absurd and the demand for intelligibility do depend upon the primordial relation of finite, cognitively functioning consciousness to objects which at once present and require the ideal of immutability. This ideal is encountered; it is given and is the condition that permits consciousness to reflect on itself and its object. The relationship is recognized at the moment of reflection that affirms conscious activity and that in turn acknowledges identity or Form against which consciousness itself can be recognized.

The incongruity and unintelligibility of the relationship between consciousness and Form is ineradicable. Consciousness does not create the incongruity between itself and immutable Form. Nor is the absurdity of this relationship dependent simply on the incapacity of consciousness to achieve its ideal. Both consciousness and Form are underived with respect to each other. Neither is a product of the other. Consciousness discovers itself within the relation of itself to Form. It is given simultaneously as one mode of unstable being with its other, the mode of stable being. Thus, the model that comes from the tradition is not an arbitrary construction. It is given, just as the instability of finite consciousness is given, and it cannot be abandoned. The identification of what confronts consciousness, the identification of consciousness itself, depends upon the traditional model of intelligibility that construes what is known in terms of an identity and thus of a Form. And it is the inescapability of this model as well as the finitude of consciousness which is the second locus of the fundamentally absurd.

C. THE SECOND MODEL OF INTELLIGIBILITY

Thus far, the absurd has been described in the light of the contrast between radical change and Form. At this point, therefore, we must consider whether the absurd is intelligible in terms of the aesthetic model of intelligibility suggested by metaphorical expression. It was said that creations are intelligible when regarded from the perspective of unmediated apprehension. This affirmation of intelligibility implies that aesthetic understanding presupposes a model of intelligibility other than the model which relies on Form.

In order to show as clearly as possible what is at stake, it will perhaps be helpful to notice further what is meant by the term "model of intelligibility" and, in this connection, to summarize the two models that have been considered. Up to this point, I have taken for granted that the term "a model of intelligibility" refers to the expectations proper to a kind of understanding. More exactly, a model is a set of characteristics that are presupposed as a basis for affirming the presence of something. The set of characteristics has a normative function and serves as a standard to be met. A model of intelligibility is the standard to which what is intelligible must conform. Accordingly, it is also a standard to which not only the object that is intelligible, but also the act of intelligence, must conform. Unless the cognitive act were controlled by the standard of intelligibility, it would miss the intelligibility of its object. And unless the object conformed to the standard, it would not be intelligible. On the first model of intelligibility, the standard is a Form that is relevant to and exemplified by the object that is intelligible. The object must be apprehended by virtue of an identity without which the object would, at most, be an indiscriminate or indeterminate manifold.

This general characterization of the model implies three component requirements that function together. The identity that renders an object intelligible must be isolable in the sense that it is distinct and manifest. Further, the identity makes possible connections which may be either inferences or additional identities necessitated by the Form. What is intelligible must in principle be realizable in other presentations. A general identity such as a law or regularity in human behavior – the disposition to desire pleasure, for example – is the basis for inferences about human behavior. A mathematical identity such as a geometrical object – triangularity, for instance – necessitates the identity of other mathematical identities: figure, as well as point, line, angle, etc. Finally, the identity, as distinct and relevant beyond its moment of manifestation, must be other than what it is not. It must be an identity in difference from other identities and from indeterminateness.

What, by contrast, are the normative characteristics or requirements of the second model? The first requirement is non-discrete presence. The object must be given as a discernible presentation; it is present as a discriminated field for apprehension. Yet the object is bounded, but its boundaries are not fixed "lines." Its boundaries are located by the intensities of relevance of the various components of the object to the central focus of the presentation. The second requirement is immediacy. The object must be immediately available; it is not the result of an inference, nor is it a term in a connection – though, of course, it may be regarded this way later, in accord with the first model. Further, the object must not offer its intelligibility by virtue of discursively available and isolated parts discriminable within it. Whatever internal relatedness it has, it is not the connections or terms in connection taken discretely which ground its intelligibility. Thus, the third requirement is that the intelligible object must have non-conceptual coherence. This coherence is given in the focus of the presentation, in an integration, and it is apprehended directly, in a non-discursive act. As intelligible in its own terms, its components are constituents rather than antecedent or consequent elements. The presence of these components functioning constitutively is a necessary condition for the presence of discontinuity (the inner and outer negativity) that enables us to recognize a different or new intelligibility in the object. Finally, the model requires that there be difference in time, or that change be present. The presence of change is evident in the difference between constituents and abstractable elements. Such a difference may lead to a static comparison between discriminated identities, but it is itself not merely a difference between items given simultaneously for attention. It is a difference discernible by virtue of recognized transmutation of items. It is present in the contrast between antecedent elements and these antecedent elements transmuted, and both of these contrasted with the consequent elements. This transmutation includes a temporal condition. It is such temporal contrast that grounds the appearance of newness; difference between present and past intelligibility.[9]

---

[9] It should be observed that this way of formulating the proposal for a second model of intelligibility has certain obvious affinities with Henri Bergson's view that the poet or artist directly apprehends the *élan vital,* or dynamic reality, from which intellectual, conceptual thinking derives its data. See his *An Introduction to Metaphysics,* translated by T. E. Hulme (New York: Liberal Arts Press, 1955), *The Creative Mind, op. cit.,* and *Creative Evolution,* translated by Arthur Mitchell (New York: Henry Holt, 1911). For Bergson, intuition is required in order to "know" the creative force which undergirds phenomena that are subsequently made intelligible in terms of what I have called the traditional model. Moreover, on Bergson's view, the language which is appropriate to intuition is metaphorical. It seems, then, that Bergson finds two kinds of intelligibility in something like the two models I have proposed.

However, there is a difference between what I have suggested and what Bergson has written about so well. On my proposal, the traditional model of intelligibility carries more weight than it does for Bergson. I do not see how the second model can be looked to as either necessary or meaningful except through the tension or inner conflict among identities or concepts appropriate to the first model. Bergsonian intuition alone cannot discern these identities as Forms as they are presented in tension, nor can intuition alone discriminate the discontinuities of radical change, since these erupt within definite boundaries. Discursive inquiry discloses its own limits, and the unfulfilled demands it makes brings into focus the spontaneity that requires a second model. Bergson, then, does not give as significant a role as I do to conceptual thinking, and he does not emphasize the discontinuous character of finite consciousness – a dis-

Now it might be thought that on the aesthetic model, the absurd does not arise. This model does not require that what is intelligible abide as a stable identity. Rather, it requires that intelligibility be present immediately in change or in the becoming of structure. Accordingly, consciousness in cognitive activity is not radically different from the standard of intelligibility of its object, since it attends to instances of radical change and thus participates in a relation to its object that does not require it to conform to what is other than itself in its temporal existence. Further, if the second model of intelligibility is accepted, the two models together might be thought to account somehow for the two poles of the opposition between Form and temporal discontinuity. However, I wish to suggest that fundamental absurdity also appears in spite of the acceptance of this second model. In order to show why I make this claim, we need only ask about the relationship between the two models. What, if anything, renders this relationship intelligible?

To pursue this question, I should like to expand what has been said about aesthetic intelligibility and metaphor first by making use of the most readily illustrative kind of aesthetic creation, music. In considering music, we can see how fundamental absurdity is present even within the model appealed to in aesthetic intelligibility. The patterns of sound that constitute a musical composition, to be sure, may be conceived on the traditional ideal which would call for understanding in terms of attention to the musical pattern viewed as conceptual relationships of meter, repeated melodies, harmonic support, and for some interpreters, qualities correlated with emotions and extra-musical ideas. Such analysis would be comparable to the discrimination of parts of a metaphor regarded as antecedents and perhaps consequent elements. But if the piece of music is apprehended in terms of heard qualities, that is, as a musical object whose constituents function in temporal concreteness, it is not exhausted by this kind of intelligibility. It defies conceptual intelligibility because its structure is paradoxical. The paradox here, of course, has been considered

---

continuity given to an agency that demands continuity and identity as well as change in duration.

This contrast with Bergson can also be seen in the specific characterization of metaphor which I have suggested. As already pointed out, in order that metaphorical language perform the function of articulating a kind of understanding of spontaneity, it must include negation in the form of tensions – a tension between at least two Forms or meanings. This point reflects the first point of difference, because it implies that metaphorical language depends upon the traditional model of intelligibility as the specific design that compels interpretive penetration of the conflicting meanings to the new meaning. Bergson's view does not call for this intimate connection between conceptual structure and intuitively apprehended meaning.

before in various ways. However, it is in music. I think, that the paradoxical relation of Form to structure is most sharply seen.

The musical structure exemplifies a Form that transcends the concrete presentation of structure. The Form exemplified is transcedent insofar as it governs the musical components. The score may serve as a sign of this Form. As trancendent, the Form serves as a general principle of coherence that enables the listener to sustain awareness of the connections among the passing sounds. At the same time, however, the Form must be relevant to the music as immanent; it must be integral to the structure which is exhibited. The score is meaningful with reference to virtual sounds. If the Form of the composition were not intimately relevant to its structure, as immanent or internal to the progression of sounds, the composition could not be said to have coherence. The meaning of the music, what gives coherence to the piece, would be different from the concrete work. It would not make a difference, then, whether the score indicated what could be played in a performance. In terms of aesthetic theory, this is to say that form and content, or form and matter, would be separated. The meaning of music *qua* music would not be relevant to sounds, but it would be an abstract universal, cognizable apart from possible performances, and the specific concrete elements would be expendable. In one sense, this is possible, as I have said in speaking of the transcendence of Form. But in this other sense which is demanded by full musical expectations, the transcendence without co-present immanence of intelligibility must be rejected. Somehow in music, the principle of coherence that requires each sound in definite patterns must itself be required by these specific sounds as they occur in their patterns.[10] This paradox of Form in music both illustrates and reaffirms one of the grounds for claiming that radical creativity is paradoxical. An instance of Novelty Proper is an instance of confrontation of a new structure and a newly exemplified Form, and in a creation, a Form which is confronted for the first time must first be discerned by virtue of the structure or complex of concrete patterns and details of the created product.

The reason for referring to this paradox here is to point to the fact that in the apprehension of a musical composition, we are presented with something which, although intelligible in its own terms, is nevertheless paradoxical. Thus, the aesthetic experience of music concerns an object

---

[10] A more extended discussion of this point, with consideration of its consequences for aesthetic experience and criticism, is offered in my "Intradiction: An Interpretation of Aesthetic Experience," *The Journal of Aesthetics and Art Criticism*, XXII, No. 3 (Spring, 1974), 249-261.

of attention which in its concreteness is in some sense intelligible, but this intelligibility lies in patterns which paradoxically exhibit tensions that constitute discontinuities and that are at once immanent and transcendent. What is made possible on the second model of intelligibility is acceptance of the absurd, or of the inevitable paradox which is presented in the aesthetic object.

However, as I have insisted earlier, adoption of the second model does not mean we can abandon the first. Not only is Form integral to the recognition of Novelty Proper, and thus to the apprehension of metaphors, and to an aesthetic response to music, but Form is also integral to the life of consciousness. To reiterate: aesthetic intelligibility does not replace but rather supplements the first model. Although human consciousness is finite, it also strives to transcend itself in its finitude. Its very existence includes an intentionality or activity of being directed toward some object or field which confronts its attention and which is other than it. At the same time, since it is consciousness, and not just a blind vector force such as might be attributed to some physical object, it carries with itself at least an implicit awareness of an identity other than what it intends. It is at least implicity reflective and reflexive. Consciousness, then, carries both an acknowledgment of its own finitude in temporal modifications and a demand for stability in being directed toward an other – a determinate object which is confronted as an identity in the midst of variation. Finite consciousness needs both models of intelligibility: that of the tradition, requiring immutable Form, and a second, requiring the manifestation of transition and paradox. The first is needed as a basis for making an identity relevant to consciousness for the sake of the security of stable determination; the second is needed to do justice to the undeniable and meaningful presence of change and finitude.

But the need for both models again reveals fundamental paradox, here in the context of human existence. The appropriateness and necessity of the two models reveals the absurd, the inevitable presence of Form and Formlessness, of eternality and change – in one determinate being. Both ideals are appropriate to human consciousness. And because human consciousness needs both, the absurd is present in human existence.

There is yet another peculiarity about consciousness in its demand for these two different criteria of intelligibility; and in this additional peculiarity, the paradox of human existence reappears. This can be seen if we ask whether consciousness itself might not constitute a resolution of the paradox. Why can we not say that consciousness is the carrier of a higher intelligibility, just as Form and change are carriers that accord with the first and second models respectively? In order to recognize both ideals, both kinds of intelligibility, finite consciousness must transcend them. It must exist in such a way as to enable a comparison of them and to yield an awareness of its own reflective activity in doing so. But is this transcendence itself intelligible? Short of some third ideal of intelligibility, the intelligibility of a relationship between the two models cannot be achieved. This is to say that unless there is a third model that transcends what is intelligible on the first two – that transcends both being and becoming – man as an intelligence, transcendent of both sides of his existence, is unintelligible. On the one hand, from the perspectives of these first two models, a transcendence of them would be to negate both Form and process. On the other hand, if such transcendence cannot be effected, then the only way this kind of distance from Form and process is possible for finite man is for him to exist by vacillating between temporal existence and a striving to conform as a knower to atemporal being, or Form.

The hope of specifying a more comprehensive kind of intelligibility should not be a hope for a reaffirmation of the first model in another form. We should not expect to identify a *logos* that transforms the vacillation between models into a dialectic of inner necessity. Such a developmental principle would deny the concrete finitude and individuality which is one pole of the human condition and which is integral to radical creativity. Thus, given the two models of intelligibility, intelligence can only strive to overcome the tension between the first two models of intelligibility and what they make intelligible through a "passage" back and forth between process and permanence. And this passage is carried out in a way that does not eliminate paradox. Whatever the activity of understanding the two models as they contrast with one another, this activity is neither Form nor sheer change. If it were sheer change, it would be without determinateness. If it were only Form, it would be without finitude and process. Hence it must appear inevitably as unintelligible in terms of both models of intelligibility.

Is there some third way, some third intelligible principle, which can embrace this paradox, remaining open to the polar opposites and the vacillation between them? Is there a way of understanding which neither is exhausted by the standards of Form and of spontaneity nor is dependent on a third standard that overcomes the contrast in some higher synthesis – a synthesis that, after all, falls back on the need for unity and thus the identity required by the first model?

D. THE POSSIBILITY OF A THIRD MODEL OF INTELLIGIBILITY

The first and second models of intelligibility constitute two poles standing in tension. If this tension is final and limiting on what we can expect of intelligibility, then we are committed to a dualism. One of the consequences of such a dualism for inquiry would be that we must cease to inquire with the hope of progress of some sort in the attempt to advance understanding of a world which includes creativity and fundamental absurdity. This consequence must be resisted. Philosophical reflection cannot rest at a terminus which is both incomplete and disjointed. If human intelligence must vacillate between two models of intelligibility, so long as philosophical inquiry persists, it cannot rest with vacillation alone. Its continuance demands a pursuit of increasingly comprehensive and ideally complete understanding, and the drive to understand calls for some way of taking into account the tension and the vacillation between the two models such that they are integral to the goal of comprehensiveness. The direction of inquiry must be toward a goal that satisfies the requirements of both sides of the cognitive function of consciousness so that these may function together in a life of cognition that overcomes fragmentation without denying the inevitability of tension. In this final section, and in conclusion, I shall suggest a way in which such an aim can be approached at the same time that the need to vacillate between the two models of intelligibility is not rejected. In other words, I shall indicate the requirements that a third model of intelligibility needs to meet, though I shall not thereby affirm the possibility of completely successful realization of such a model.

In order to see what can be expected of a third kind of intelligibility, it is appropriate to begin by reconsidering the purposes that prompt and give direction to inquiry. Specifically, it will be necessary to ask about what purposes might lie behind an inquiry undertaken in the face of the acknowledgment of the tension between conceptual structure and radically creative process. What purposes may underlie and guide an inquiry that accepts both models?

Since some if not all of these purposes may be shared with those who study creativity but who do not afirm its radical character, it will be helpful first to consider briefly those purposes that are generally presupposed by inquiry. A consideration of the general purposes of inquiry, of course, is a major study in its own right. The present discussion will be limited to what I believe are the principal assumptions underlying these purposes, particularly as these seem relevant to our specific topic.

One of the most widely held purposes of inquiry is to find ways either to nurture or to prevent the phenomenon under study. Certainly, a large number of studies of creativity spring from the hope of stimulating and cultivating it. This purpose is particularly evident in the investigations reported by educational psychologists. Educators in general have been interested in learning how to detect and foster creativity in students. Nurturing creativity also clearly lies behind the theoretical and clinical work of many psychoanalysts. On the one hand, insight into creativity may provide a basis for a better understanding of normal behavior. On the other hand, psychotherapy seems to require some form of creative effort from the patient or the therapist (psychoanalyst or clinical psychologist) or both, and one expectation of investigating creativity is that creative therapy can be fostered.

Achievement of the goal of nurtering creativity, however, depends upon at least some degree of success in realizing a theoretical purpose: identifying what are ordinarily called "causes," or general principles that necessitate or are at least correlated with creative achievement. This point is important, because it shows that realization of the practical goal depends upon some theoretical understanding, and the limitations on theoretical inquiry imply limitations on our practical expectations. I should like to look more closely at the relation of practical to theoretical purposes, emphasizing the senses in which both may consist in a search for causes. Although it will be necessary to cover some of the same ground covered earlier, my aim is to focus on causes here in order to elicit certain criteria appropriate to a third model of intelligibility.

As I have indicated already, contemporary discussions admit the possibility of two kinds of causes, efficient and final. Efficient causes are generally identified in terms of necessary and sufficient antecedent conditions for the occurrence of what is to be explained. These conditions include, or at least must be connected with, general laws and specific circumstances which are expected to be present when the phenomenon to be explained occurs. Accordingly, a major test of whether such causes are known is successful prediction. Thus, the purpose of discovering efficient causes may be subordinated to the further purpose of predicting – a purpose that flows from the need man has to control his environment.

The requirement of prediction as integral to explanation, of course, has been an important consideration in earlier sections of this book, specifically in the criticisms of those approaches that presuppose that creativity is explicable in terms of gaining foreknowledge of instances of creativity. But we can now see that understanding in order to make predictions assumes a model of intelligibility that calls for identifying something invariant in the midst of difference.[11] Accordingly, the inquirer may focus on such identities or repeatable connections, without concern for making actual predictions. He might concentrate on the ground of the predictions rather than on the predictions themselves. But this concern is directed away from merely practical purposes made possible by prediction. One's aim then would be primarily theoretical: understanding the principles to which predictions are subordinate and in accordance with which predicted occurrences might be viewed as components integral to a system that satisfies intellectual curiosity. Ideally, intelligent theoretical curiosity would seek understanding of a general system comprehensive of all events, past, present, and future. In short, I am saying that practical purposes of finding causes of phenomena presuppose theoretical purposes which may be regarded as the primary concern of inquiry, and the full realization of such purposes finds completion in a comprehensive system of principles, which in its ideal form, is a complete whole from which no explanatory principle or phenomenon to be explained is absent.

Now it should be obvious that on the view presented in this book, the purpose of understanding creative acts by focusing on efficient causes of effects can at best be fulfilled only partially. Neither complete predictability of, nor exhaustive analysis of connections with, radical creativity can be achieved. Nevertheless, there is a sense in which the admission of radical creativity in conjunction with the search for efficient causes may serve, on the one hand, certain limited practical purposes of inquiry and, on the other hand, certain qualified theoretical purposes. As a methodological assumption, determinism may serve practically as a guiding conceptual framework that justifies the pursuit of causal explanation. Yet it is equally important to keep in mind the limitation of this framework as an adequate theory. The framework must be seen in its function as primarily a stimulus to practical ends which may be unrealizable for some phenomena.

Let me pursue this point for a moment in order to suggest a way in which it has certain practical consequences. The possibility of reaching practical goals of inquiry depends upon accepting the limitations of

---

[11] Peirce saw this and made it the basis for that component of realism which treated generals as operative in nature. Thus, he argued that the precedence in experience of certain continuities and the successful prediction of events the likes of which occurred in the past could only be accounted for by the independent reality of generals. See *Colleted Papers of Charles Sanders Peirce, op. cit.,* Vol. V, Paragraphs 93-107.

theoretical understanding and incorporating within our practical purposes an acknowledged restriction on the aim of explaining creativity by tracing it to antecedents and making it predictable. If the purpose of exhaustive analysis and prediction cannot be fully realized, then inquiries had better direct themselves in terms of restricted purposes. Let me emphasize that this is not to recommend abandoning the search for causes altogether. The determinist presupposition has its own heuristic value. But I do want to recommend that the main approach of such a search should be aimed at what circumscribes rather than exhausts the phenomenon to be explained. Thus, one may search for motives and repeatable patterns in the personalities of creative persons. Success in identifying these would provide information and necessary (though not sufficient) conditions under which creative acts could occur. While such success would not yield specific predictive power, it would provide certain negative results. It would surely throw light on the motives and personalities of persons whom we do not expect to be radically creative. If we were to know the conditions that are necessary (though not sufficient) for creativity, and if these conditions were not present, we could predict with some degree of probability that a person or act will not be creative. At the same time, the acknowledged limitation on understanding creativity should keep us alert to the possibility that the prediction is only probable. We might be surprised. Yet unless we are, our most reasonable approach would be either to foster further necesary conditions for the person in question or to look elsewhere for creative achievement.

In general, however, the acknowledgment that there are limitations on understanding creativity has a value which, though negative, is at least also heuristic: it suggests that some of our inquiries be directed away from ends impossible to realize and toward different, perhaps less ambitious ends. If it be said that I have overlooked the fact that contemporary philosophical and scientific purposes do operate in accord with such acknowledged limitations – we are no longer subject to Newtonian physics or to rationalistic and deterministic programs – I must emphasize that acknowledgment of these limits of inquiry is not made explicit in most approaches to creativity. Nor has an ontology been envisaged which takes both conceptual intelligibility and discontinuity into a balanced account. In any case, it is this turn in the expectations of practical understanding that suggests how the admission of radical novelty may serve theoretical purposes. Theoretical as well as practical inquiry about creativity presupposes a modification of our purposes.[12]

[12] This recommendation that we shift our explanatory aims is consistent with some

But suppose that inquiry is concerned not principally with efficient causes but with final causes. In that case, what consequences for inquiry follow? The pursuit of understanding goal-directed activity or finding final causes implies a willingness to entertain the possibility of a teleological framework for explanation. A teleology need not exclude efficient causal relations; but it takes in more, for it attempts to design a system within which components are inferrable without respect to exclusive attention to temporally antecedent data. A teleology entertains possibilities at least some of which are realizable in the future, as well as actualities already realized and standing in the system as antecedents.

The adoption of teleological explanation, then, implies an acceptance of the limitation of efficient causes in explaining certain occurrences in the world.[13] However, the arguments offered in previous chapters also affirm limitations on a teleological understanding of a world in which there are instances of radical novelty. It was suggested that inquiry would be satisfied with teleological understanding in the most comprehensive sense only if it were to reach an exhaustive identification of interconnected and coherently related final causes that cover all occurrences in the world. It is true that, in a narrower sense, inquiry might restrict itself and be satisfied with identifying goals for particular actions and the means to those goals. But in both the narrow and the comprehensive sense, the purpose of teleological understanding is to discover ends and means, or goals and the development of processes required for the sake of the goals. This aim is satisfied if the discovered means and ends are identifiable in

---

of the proposals offered by writers who belong to a different perspective than the one I represent. For instance, modification of theoretical purposes can be seen in recent discussions of human behavior. Lack of success in making complete predictions and acknowledgement of the limitations of explanation serves as a basis for the willingness on the part of some inquirers today to admit the relevance of final causality as well as efficient causality for explanation. For example, in a book devoted to the problems of understanding human behavior in relation to freedom of choice, Richard Taylor says: "... in case certain typical human behavior is purposeful, as it most certainly is, then it will follow that much of the science of human behavior is simply on the wrong track." Richard Taylor, *Action and Purpose* (Englewood Cliffs, New Jersey: Prentice Hall, Inc., 1966), p. 204. His assertion is based on two premises: the first is that experimental psychology assumes that human behavior is understandable in terms of observable and verifiable evidence and that it is predictable; the second is that human actions are goal directed and spring from choices which are not predictable in terms of antecedent or efficient causality. If Taylor's statement is representative of a change in contemporary conceptions of inquiry, then the recommendation I am suggesting shares common ground with the thought of those not committed as I am to the insistence on radical creativity.

[13] I here use the term "occurrences" with a special meaning — to take into account a distinction made in some of the current literature. The term covers both *events* (or behavior), which are thought of as subject to efficient causal relations, and *acts*, which are thought of as connected in some way with an agent and as eluding complete analysis by means of efficient causal relations.

a system or coherent scheme, whether the system were to embrace either a metaphysical whole or a restricted part of a possible whole.

Again, however, this aim is thwarted to the extent that radical creativity is present in the occasions or actions we wish to understand. As already argued, the creative act originates the purpose or end at which it aims, and the origination of the end determines what means are appropriate. We can at best distinguish such means and ends only after their origin. Consequently, if a comprehensive teleological system is sought, this system must be discontinuously developmental. It must be incomplete, even as an ideal, for it must include discontinuities and gaps in the connections among final causes as well as in the processes that lead to these. If a developmental teleological explanation is relevant to creative acts, it must be a level of explanation which circumscribes particular inexplicable acts and fits them into a large scheme which nevertheless accepts them as inexplicable because they elude the continuities of the scheme. Such an explanation would have the practical value of supporting inquiry about efficient causes. Identifying fundamental and comprehensive laws and principles formulated in terms of goals can throw light on which antecedent conditions are relevant to creative acts in general.[14] Most important at the practical level would be to study the relationships of the various kinds of values creators have affirmed and have rejected before and after creativity. The role of the value of simply bringing something into being, regardless of what it is, in the development and generation of specific values before and after creation would surely make clearer what conditions, unacknowledged as well as envisaged, are relevant to creative acts. Though I do not think success in this undertaking would yield predictions such as may be found in non-creative human behavior, I do suggest that success would narrow the range of surprises we should expect from creative individuals. And to narrow this range would enable society to accept more readily those surprises in creations that are the lifeblood of cultures.

Whatever practical hopes may be assigned to the construction of a developmental teleology, this kind of explanation can meet a purely theoretical purpose of understanding a world that includes creativity. But if this is so, the intelligibility of the teleology must be open to the two kinds of intelligibility already outlined. Can such understanding successfully

---

[14] Arthur Koestler's *The Act of Creation, op. cit.*, nicely illustrates an attempt to interweave teleological with mechanistic considerations. Purposive activity is related to genetic coding and environmental triggering. However, more attention is needed to the larger teleological framework presupposed by Koestler. I have argued this in "Understanding and the Act of Creation," *The Review of Metaphysics*, XX, No. 1 (September, 1966), 88-112.

bring together the requirements of the two models of intelligibility? In other words, does discontinuous developmental teleology presuppose a third model of intelligibility that does not exclude the first two?

I think this question can be answered affirmatively, though with certain crucial qualifications. A discontinuous developmental teleology may embrace what is understood on the two models and hold both in a single comprehensive view. Moreover, this view should not – cannot, short of collapsing into a determinism – overcome the tension between radical change and Form. The perspective of the third model presupposed by discontinuous developmental teleology must include the others in their own terms. From the perspective of these models held together, an increment of unintelligibility remains. The *contrast* between them is not intelligible in terms of either model. This situation, it seems, is inevitable, because the two models that are brought together are opposites: they oppose one another with respect to what counts as intelligible in terms of either of them. As such, they cannot stand in harmony on their own terms. The hope of an dequate developmental teleology must then acknowledge the fundamental conflict, that is, epistemically, the tension between the two ideals of intelligibility and, ontologically, the tension between what is known in accord with these models. Such acknowledgment consists in a contemplative vision of fundamental opposites, each intelligible in a different way.

Because of the tension within the third model, there is reason to compare it with one of the poles of the tension: the second, and what is apprehended in accord with this model, namely, that which appears with tensions appropriately understood aesthetically. Indeed, understanding on a third model, which takes in the first two models of intelligibility, seems strikingly close to the aim of aesthetic understanding; and we may seem to have given a priority to the second model, or to aesthetic understanding. Both require a contemplative regard for what is intelligible, and both require assent to tension. However, there is a difference between this third kind of understanding and aesthetic understanding. First of all, if the contemplation or understanding that conforms to the possible third model were realized, it would include as a pole what is manifest and in that sense is an identity of atemporal identities in contrast with discontinuous process. The conceptual and the anti-conceptual poles are envisaged in balance. Understanding on the aesthetic model, by contrast, is directed primarily toward change and the discontinuous. Conceptualizable, stable order enters into and has its significance within aesthetic understanding only in terms of marking the difference of what is understood from what was established.

Witness of radical change, then, is central, to this model, while apprehension of structure is the framework that makes this possible. But the model of intelligibility of contemplative vision requires equal emphasis on both radical change and atemporal identity. Atemporal identity is not the means to witnessing radical change. Nor is radical change an avenue to reconstituting Form. This point emphasizes the difference between my view and most, if not all, intuitionist's views (such as that of Bergson) or a theory that affirms a superior cognitive act (such as that of some forms of idealism). On such views, the third model would be aesthetic understanding raised to intuition of reality or to a supra-rational knowledge of fundamental unity. But on my view, conceptualized reality and radical change both hold their places within the vision. Contemplative vision accepts the tension between stable Form and discontinuity. Tension is sustained. The superior cognition of idealism and the non-conceptual cognition of intuitionism eradicate radical differences and the tension they exhibit. The contemplative vision that includes radical creativity must embrace disorder within established order, and the discontinuous has its significance as carrying its own weight within the framework of established structure.

Further, what is contemplated on this third model is not an object, at least in the sense of a determinate confrontation for cognitive consciousness. What is contemplated is dynamic – simultaneously stable and unstable, complete as determinate but incomplete in its other side, as what endures in radical change. This side is the manifestation of unbounded and indefinitely persistent spontaneity.

Moreover, what is contemplated, while having a cue in aesthetic objects, is not an aesthetic object, because it is not finite. The world is not an aesthetic object, or a bounded completed whole that is given purely to be appreciated. Although aesthetic objects manifest change and are incomplete insofar as they reveal indefinite richness, they are finite as controlled by their structures which are controlling centers that give the objects focus. What is contemplated on the third model is not finite; rather it is the basis of indefinitely numerous variations that may erupt in finite contexts.

Although the third model must be distinguished from the other models, the intelligibility of the third is implicit in them both. The identity required in conceptualization is a harbinger of the identity of what is envisaged in contemplative vision. In aesthetic understanding, both identity in difference or structure and discontinuous and changing elements are embraced. Thus, in aesthetic objects we encounter bounded and individual instances that suggest in an anticipatory way what is to be understood at the most fundamental level with respect to the world.

But is this third model only an ideal? The qualification of the third model that it must include tension serves as a reminder of the argument that because of the limitations on human intelligence, inquiry can only vacillate between conceptual and immediate knowledge. On the basis of the argument presented earlier in this chapter, it seems that because of the finitude of the inquirer, the ideal of the third model of intelligibility is impossible. What might be a comprehensive act of contemplation necessarily collapses into a vacillation between the two poles of the other models. Such vacillation seems to conflict with the aim of contemplation, that is, the goal of the third kind of understanding which calls for the contemplator's resting in a comprehensive vision of what is contemplated. Finite consciousness has been characterized as what cannot thus remain steadfast in an enduring state. If a third model is possible, then, it must embrace not only order and disorder, but it also must include a vacillation between these. At the same time, because it is a contemplative understanding, it is non-discursive and not limited to a moment or series of moments in a linear time sequence. Consequently, it must collapse the vacillation it includes so that it takes the two poles into account simultaneously. Thus the contemplative understanding must nullify the temporal passage entailed by the activity of vacillating. Such contemplation cancels the time interval of alternating between the intelligibilities of Form and discontinuous change. This must be done without at the same time cancelling the understanding on the second model of radical change which itself is constituted with reference to time.

The possibility of realizing an understanding on this third model implies three further points. First, we should see that the final goal of understanding reached in a contemplation telescopes the vacillation between Form and discontinuity and reaffirms the fundamental paradox or absurdity insisted upon earlier. It reveals again the need for acceptance and assent to paradox. If this assent is affirmed, we have prepared the way for a kind of understanding that appropriately includes both the first and second models of intelligibility as these serve in making intelligible a world that includes both continuity and discontinuity.

There is a second point associated with the possibility of realizing contemplative vision. It is important to keep in mind that the three kinds of understanding under discussion are based on models, that is, ideals of intelligibility. As models, the intelligibility expected in each instance of understanding is approximated. Thus, the models are ideals that may not be completely realized or actualized. However, what is understood stands under one or other model of intelligibility which serves as an ideal condition. The third model, then, is the condition under which the tension between the other two models is intelligible – intelligible in a third way. The ideal limit of this condition is the temporal telescoping without loss of tension in a contemplative comprehension in simultaneity of the two opposing poles.

The third and final point implied by the proposal that a third model of intelligibility may be entertained as a possibility concerns one fundamental criterion common to all three models. This has been hinted at above in the observation that the first two models presage the third. There is a standard common to both conceptual and aesthetic understanding: namely, the requirement that what is intelligible on either model must be manifest. The intelligible must be revealed in a presence. Insofar as it is given as a presence, what is intelligible is not a specific or particular identity with ideally precise unity or boundaries, nor is it an immediately given transmutation. It is true that a specific concern about something which is intelligible must attend to definiteness or to change known by acquaintance, depending upon which model plays a dominant role. But the condition of being present is the condition that either Form or radical change be manifest. Manifestation or being present is being given in focus, whether the focus is that of a transmuting or of a controlling center of structure and Form. Being manifest, or being given as a presence, is shared by intelligibility under both models. This shared standard is the fundamental criterion of the third model. Contemplative vision is an open, indeterminate, directed surveying of a manifestation. The manifestation contains polarity and tension, but it is nevertheless a manifestation. What is present under this model is not present as a particular identity, but it is "something" unbounded by conceptual limits and inclusive of transmutation that is manifest.

I should like to conclude by returning briefly to the question of the relevance of inquiry to practical concerns. Just as the demand of inquiry points to a third model of intelligibility, so the third model is suggestive for a way of approaching practical concerns in inquiry. I wish to point out that the non-practical, theoretical purpose of understanding in accord with the third model carries with it a correlative, practical end, a practical purpose which theoretical understanding may serve. Just as there is the possibility of finding a restricted explanation in terms of efficient causality by circumscribing creative acts, there is the possibility of constructing a teleological understanding under the standards of the third model of intelligibility which acknowledges recalcitrant discontinuities. This understanding does not simply call for the negative approach of looking for necessary conditions and abandoning the search for sufficient conditions. Rather, it calls for confronting creative acts as self-determined. The appropriate teleology, again, is discontinuous in being developmental. Creative acts, as self-determined, generate their own goals, and inquiry must concern itself with the conditions connected with these unpredictable goals. Thus, as already pointed out, a particular inquiry aimed at finding causes may discover goals that are correlated exclusively with creative acts in contrast with routine processes. The identification of these goals might be incorporated within a science of mental processes. But, further, particular inquiries and special sciences may be taken up in more comprehensive inquiry. These would include teleological accounts of moral and aesthetic kinds of activities, both creative and non-creative. On the second model of intelligibility, such inquiry would be one-sided, in emphasizing the demands of inquiry for stability. On the first model of intelligibility, such special inquires would be incomplete, lacking in the demand for enduring identity and full coherence. But a special inquiry need be thought incomplete or one-sided only if its purpose is construed as doing justice to one or the other models of intelligibility. If the inquirer could rest content (as I have suggested that one constructing an ontology must) with the entertainment of breaks and gaps in the scheme, the inquirer could be credited with success in his own terms.

Finally, this more general purpose, patterned on the third model of intelligibility, also has heuristic value. The third model of understanding points the way to acceptance of tension. But more specifically, we are directed toward an approach to creativity that searches for conditions of unpredictable goals in paradoxical situations – situations that include events or experiences that manifest internal oppositions and external oppositions with their pasts. Acordingly, practical inquiry can be directed toward finding specific oppositions which are at once unique and necessary conditions of creativity.

The theoretical or philosophical model that guides intelligence, however, is neither the model of Form nor of change. Indeed, it is not a model in the sense that conceptualization and aesthetic acquaintance imply models. The third way of understanding is more like a way of regarding a paradoxical world. It is a way of being cognitively open to a world apprehended as an unbounded metaphor.

INDEX

absurd, the, 125–138, 143
accident, 41–44
acquaintance, *see* cognition
actual being, actual unity, *see* actuality
actuality, actual/ideal being, 51, 65, 135; actual/ideal unity, 31
aesthetic experience, *see* Forms
aesthetic object, *see* work of art *under* art
Alexander, Samuel, 61
Aristotle, 4, 25, 27, 57, 81, 94, 99–100, 103, 111, 128, 135
art, viii, 1, 4–5, 11, 16, 49, 50, 97–99, 115–116, 122; art proper 28; artistic tradition, 90; Baroque art, 90; Egyptian art, 40–41; German Expressionism, 23; Impressionism, 29; Oriental art, 40; Post-Impressionism, 23; Romanticism, 1; work of art, 14–15, 23–24, 25–26, 49, 95–99, 116, 152; *see also* music, painting, poetry
art proper, *see* art
artistic tradition, *see* art

Bach, Johann Sebastian, 49
Barfield, Owen, 90, 99
Baroque art, *see* art
Beardsley, Monroe C., 99, 101, 105
Beethoven, van, Ludwig, 15, 45, 116
Bergmann, Gustav, 28, 70
Bergson, Henri, 72, 81–84, 140–141, 152
Blanshard, Brand, 56, 73
Bradley, A. C., 61

Camus, Albert, 127
cause, 56–59, 146; *see also* explanation
Cézanne, Paul, 23, 34, 36, 49, 98, 122
cognition, acquaintance, 121–122, 155; concepts, 10, 36, 45, 81–82; fluid concepts, 83; illumination, 98; induction, 55; inspiration, 5; intelligibility, 21–28, 32–35, 51, 53–54, 81–82, 114–155; intuition, 81, 100, 140, 152; Janusian thinking, 108–109; problem-solving, 55; true opinion, 21
Collingwood, R. G., 28, 43, 88
commanding form, *see* Forms
concepts, *see* cognition
conceptualism, 33; *see also* empiricism, existentialism, Idealism, materialism, nominalism, phenomenology, positivism, pragmatism, realism, supernaturalism
consciousness, 35, 64–65, 74–80, 84, 134–145; *see also* object
continuity, 36–39, 43, 81, 104, 120, 150; *see also* evolution, spontaneity
craftsmanship, 40–41
creating-consicousness, *see* creativity
creation *ex nihilo*, *see* creativity
creativity, vii-ix, 1–19, 26–29, 39–55, 59–68, 89–93, 95–99, 110, 114–125, 132–133, 145–155; creating-consciousness, 64–68; creation *ex nihilo*, 89, *see also* novelty
criticism, 115–116
Croce, Benedetto, 71, 96

Darwin, Charles, 44, 45
depth-psychology, *see* psychology
determinism, 3–4, 20, 53–54, 120, 147–148; mechanistic determinism, 4, 66, 74–81; positivistic determinism, 70–72; predictability 2–3, 20, 53, 58, 69, 146–148, 149, 155; teleological determinism, 59, 63–64, 65, 72–73, 149–151
Dewey, John, 24, 88

INDEX

dialectic, 84, 144
diaphoric movement, 103; *see also* metaphor
Don Quixote, 71
Dostoevski, Fyodor, 75
Dufrenne, Mikel, 99
Duns Scotus, John, 21

Edie, James, 99
educational psychology, *see* psychology
Egyptian art, *see* art
élan vital, 82, 141
element, *see* whole/part
emergence, *see* novelty
empiricism, 111; *see also* conceptualism, existentialism, Idealism, materialism, nominalism, phenomenology, positivism, pragmatism, realism, supernaturalism
evolution, 9, 28, 36, 43–44, 61, 87; *see also* continuity
existentialism, *see* the absurd; *see also* conceptualism, empircism, Idealism, materialism, nominalism, phenomenology, positivism, pragmatism, realism, supernaturalism
experimental psychology, *see* psychology
explanation, 2–6, 11–14, 29–30, 53–61, 70–80, 146–155; *see also* cause, ontology
extrinsic value, *see* value

family resemblances, 96, 110–114
fluid concepts, *see* cognition
Forms, 9, 14, 19, 21, 25–52, 69, 71, 82, 85, 86–87, 96, 98–99, 111, 115, 128–144, 151–155; form and aesthetic experience, 142–143; commanding form, 50; Gestalt, 25, 105; form and intelligibility, 21–27, 128–155; ontological status of Forms, 29, 33, 128–129
freedom, *see* spontaneity
Freud, Sigmund, 12, 74–75, 122

German Expressionism, *see* art
Gestalt, *see* Forms
Giotto di Bondone, 45, 49, 90
Good, the, 129
Greco, El, Domenico Teotocopulo, 49

Hamlet, 106
Hanson, Norwood, 45
Hartmann, Nicolai, 51, 64–68

Heccaeity, 21; *see also* individuality
Hegel, Georg Wilhelm Friedrich, 59, 73
Heidegger, Martin, 128
Henle, Paul, 28, 66, 99, 103, 105
Hume, David, 57, 58
Husserl, Edmund, 64

ideal being, ideal unity, *see* actuality
Idealism, 1, 25, 59, 121, 152; *see also* conceptualism, empiricism, existentialism, materialism, nominalism, phenomenology, positivism, pragmatism, realism, supernaturalism
ideality, *see* actuality
illumination, *see* cognition; *see also* unconscious
Impressionism, *see* art
indeterminacy principle, 69
individuality, 7, 20–29, 97
induced similarity, 103
induction, *see* cognition
inherent value, *see* value
insight, *see* illumination
inspiration, *see* cognition
instrumental value, *see* value
intelligibility, *see* cognition
intrinsic value, *see* value
intuition, *see* cognition

Janusian thinking, *see* cognition; *see also* oxymoron

Keats, John, 91, 97, 99–100
Klee, Paul, 23, 25
Koestler, Arthur, 74, 150

Langer, Susanne K., 50
language, 33, 81–96; *see also* meaning, metaphor
Leibniz, von, Baron Gottfried Wilhelm, 44, 58, 83
Lewis, C. I., 47
logos, 13; *see also* language, meaning

MacLeod, Robert B., 40
madness, 5
Maritain, Jacques, 6
Maslow, A. H., 8
materialism, 4; *see also* conceptualism, empiricism, existentialism, Idealism, nominalism, phenomenology, positivism, pragmatism, realism, supernaturalism

meaning, 15, 86–96, 101–114; *see also* language, metaphor
mechanism, *see* mechanistic determinism *under* determinism
mechanistic determinism, *see* determinism
metaphor, 17, 82–86, 93–123, 125, 155; strength and weakness of Bergson's treatment of metaphor, 82, 140–141
Michelangelo Buonaroti, 41, 90
Morgan, C. Lloyd, 28, 66
Mozart, Wolfgang Amadeus, 44, 122
music, 15, 25, 28, 30, 43, 49, 87, 91, 92, 110, 116, 122, 135, 141–142; *see also* art

Nazism, 51
Newton, Isaac, 44, 148
nominalism, 29, 33, 128–129; *see also* conceptualism, empiricism, existentialism, Idealism, materialism, phenomenology, positivism, pragmatism, realism, supernaturalism
novelty, 8–55, 59–96, 101, 116–123, 132–133, 142–143, 149; emergence of novelty, 28, 66–67; Novelty Proper, 28–49, 52–55, 59, 63–64, 70, 85, 95–96, 117, 123, 132, 142–143; primary novelty, 28; *see also* creativity
Novelty Proper, *see* novelty

object, aesthetic object, *see* work of art *under* art; object of consciousness, 26–27, 137–138, 142–143; *see also* consciousness
ontology, 52, 66, 69, 125, 133, 155; *see also* explanation
Oriental art, *see* art
oxymoron, 108–110; *see also* Janusian thinking

painting, 23–25, 28–29, 34, 36, 49, 77, 87, 90, 91, 92, 98, 110, 122; *see also* art
paradox, 3, 7, 10–17, 29, 34, 51, 64, 67–68, 91, 99, 123–155
Parmenides, 68
part/whole, *see* whole/part
Pasteur, Louis, 43, 48
Peirce, C. S., 21, 29, 59, 130, 147
phenomenology, 29–30, 54, 64–65; *see also* conceptualism, empiricism, existentialism, Idealism, materialism, nominalism, positivism, pragmatism, realism, supernaturalism

Picasso, Pablo, 49
Plato, 5, 10, 25, 27, 29, 33, 81, 83, 94, 111, 128, 129, 135
Plotinus, 81
poetry, 5, 25, 74, 82–85, 91, 93, 95, 97, 105–108; *see also* art
positivism, *see* determinism; *see also* conceptualism, empiricism, existentialism, Idealism, materialism, nominalism, phenomenology, pragmatism, realism, supernaturalism
Post-Impressionism, *see* art
pragmatism, 29, 129, 130; *see also* conceptualism, empiricism, existentialism, Idealism, materialism, nominalism, phenomenology, positivism, realism, supernaturalism
predictablity, *see* determinism
primary novelty, *see* novelty
problem-solving, *see* cognition
psychoanalytic theory, *see* psychology
psychology, 8, 12; depth-psychology, 4; educational psychology, 146; experimental psychology, vii; psychoanalytic theory, 74–80, 122
purpose, 149; *see also* will, teleological determinism *under* determinism
puzzle, *see* paradox

quantum theory, 69

realism, 33, 130, 147; *see also* conceptualism, empiricism, existentialism, Idealism, materialism, nominalism, phenomenology, positivism, pragmatism, supernaturalism
Renoir, Pierre Auguste, 28
Romanticism, *see* art
Rothenberg, Albert, 108–109
Russell, Bertrand, 71, 121

Sartre, Jean-Paul, 84, 94, 131–132
Schon, Donald, 94
Shakespeare, William, 106, 115, 122
Skinner, B. F., 4, 74, 80
Socrates, 94
Spinoza, Baruch, 3, 58, 81, 94
spontaneity, 13, 14, 36, 43, 53–81, 84, 117, 133, 152; *see also* continuity, will
Stevens, Wallace, 106–108
supernaturalism, 4, 6; *see also*, conceptualism, empiricism, existentialism, Idealism, materialism, nominalism,

phenomenology, positivism, pragmatism, realism

Taylor, Richard, 149
telological determinism, *see* determinism
tenor/vehicle, 101
Thomas Aquinas, Saint, 81
Tomas, Vincent, 43
true opinion, *see* cognition
Turbayne, Colin, 94

unconscious, 12, 98, 122
unity, 15, 31, 47, 68, 95, 97–98, 124, 144, 154
utilitarian value, *see* value

value, 19, 31–32, 46–53, 62, 67; extrinsic value, 47–48; inherent value, 47, 49–51; instrumental value, 47–49, 50; intrinsic value, 47; utilitarian value, 47–48
vehicle/tenor, *see* tenor/vehicle
Vivas, Eliseo, 61, 66, 96, 119

Wallace, A. R., 44, 45
Wallas, Graham, 43
Weitz, Morris, 96
Wheelwright, Philip, 99, 103
Whitehead, A. N., 20, 28, 60–64, 65
whole/part, 95, 97–98, 130
will, 57; *see also* spontaneity, purpose
Wittgenstein, Ludwig, 22, 81, 110–114
work of art, *see* art